A Windsor Handbook

A Windsor Handbook

Comprising Illustrations & Descriptions of
WINDSOR FURNITURE OF ALL PERIODS
including Side Chairs, Arm Chairs, Comb-Backs,
Writing-Arm Windsors, Babies' High Backs,
Babies' Low Chairs, Child's Chairs, also
Settees, Love Seats, Stools, & Tables

by WALLACE NUTTING

CHARLES E. TUTTLE COMPANY
Rutland, Vermont

Representatives

Continental Europe: BOXERBOOKS, INC., *Zurich*
British Isles: PRENTICE-HALL INTERNATIONAL, INC., *London*
Canada: HURTIG PUBLISHERS, *Edmonton*
Australasia: BOOK WISE (AUSTRALIA) PTY. LTD.
104-108 Sussex Street, Sydney 2000

Published by the Charles E. Tuttle Company, Inc.
of Rutland, Vermont & Tokyo, Japan
with editorial offices at
Suido 1-chome, 2-6, Bunkyo-ku, Tokyo, Japan

Copyright in Japan, 1973 by Charles E. Tuttle Co., Inc.

Library of Congress Catalog Card No. 73-77579

International Standard Book No. 0-8048-1105-9

First edition, 1917 by
Old America Company, Framingham and Boston
First Tuttle edition, 1973
Third printing, 1978

0272-000350-4615
PRINTED IN JAPAN

Publisher's Foreword

A Windsor chair, even to a person who does not know it by name, is perhaps more suggestive of pleasant reflections than any other article of furniture. How did this common chair receive its royal name? Legend has it that one of the royal Georges of England, seeing a chair of this type in a farmhouse near his castle, so greatly admired the beauty of its simple lines that he brought it to the attention of the court and made it fashionable.

Soon, Windsor chairs could be found in kitchen, dining room, and parlor; in bars, courtrooms, and schools. They were popular in Charles Dickens's day, as can seen from Seymour's illustrations for the *Pickwick Papers* in 1836. That they retain their immense popularity today may be attributed to the fact that they are "good mixers" and remarkably comfortable as an occasional chair.

One need only glance at the many illustrations in this charming book to see how homey, comfortable, and inviting these American Windsors really are. Nor is it difficult to understand how they captured the affection and admiration of the noted American writer Wallace Nutting, for Mr. Nutting was an antiquarian as well as a clergyman. Included among his many books was a series on various "beautiful" states.

Philadelphia was the first place of record where American Windsors were made; hence they were often referred to as "Philadelphia Windsor chairs." But like all other types, the chairs traveled, and soon they were advertised in such widely scattered places as Hartford, New York, Boston, and Vermont. In Vermont lived John White, who became famous as a Windsor chairmaker and decorator. John's mother was Annis Tuttle, of the Rutland publishing firm.

This handsome handbook, first published in 1917 when there were still many of these fine specimens extant and firsthand information was easy to come by, comprises illustrations and descriptions of Windsor furniture of the period between 1725 and 1825, including side chairs, arm chairs, comb-backs, writing-arm Windsors, babies' high backs, babies' low chairs, children's chairs, as well as settees, stools, tables, and love seats. Speaking of love, wouldn't you love to have some of these valuable antiques? Then you would be sitting pretty, for they run into the hundreds and thousands of dollars. And they are still "discovered" to this day; so this handbook could be worth many thousand times its weight in Windsors.

The final merit of the Windsor is in its beauty. Though its lines are simple, it is at its best very dignified, attractive, and decorative—and as American as apple pie.

How To Use This Book

THE descriptions of the pieces shown are in every case either under them or opposite them. First occurs the best general name or definition which we can give to the chair. The *Condition* is then stated, which term includes a description of any alterations or additions and indicates the general condition of the piece. Under the term *Merit* is an effort at an appraisal of the style of the piece. Here the relative terms used are: "The Highest," "Very High," "High," "Moderate," "Slight." These words are followed by some description of the good or bad features of the piece. Under *Date* the following graduated terms are used: "The Earliest," "Very Early," "Early," "Middle Period," "Late," "Very Late." The reader is cautioned that these terms are relative and that specific dates are omitted through the book, for after the most diligent investigation it is impossible to arrive at more precise statements. It is sometimes the case that two periods are mixed. There is no absolute standard of date. The statement of date is merely an approximation. All the periods are included between 1725 and 1825.

Under the word *Occurrence* is given the relative frequency with which the piece in question is found. There is here not so much reason for doubt though in some cases the classification may be challenged, so far as one step up or down is concerned. The terms employed are as follows: "Unique," "Extremely Rare," "Very Rare," "Rare," "Unusual," "Common."

Under *Owned by* is given the owner's name, if it is known and the owner does not object.

Besides the description of each chair by itself, various headings bearing upon the special features of WINDSORS are carried through the book.

Transitional Corner Chair

Peculiar in that the comb, usually attached with a splat, is a true WINDSOR comb, and has two spindles running down to the seat, thus suggesting the true WINDSOR. Shown as a connecting link. Nothing below the back is at all WINDSOR-like.

Date: 1710–1730?

Owned by the METROPOLITAN MUSEUM, New York.

The Windsor Chair

A WINDSOR chair, even to a person who does not know it by name, is perhaps more suggestive of pleasant reflections than any other article of furniture. No doubt its origin was humble, though a king George is reputed to have discovered it at Windsor and made it popular — a mere legend.

The WINDSOR chair is said to have been known by 1700, but that date is not supported by evidence. The earliest specimens in America are of about 1725.

The WINDSOR has held its popularity steadily for two centuries in its original or debased forms. No other style of furniture has been so persistent and kept its quiet place while other styles came and went.

The reasons are obvious. The WINDSOR is comfortable, and thus escapes a charge to the contrary made against most styles of antique furniture. To be sure, a common wooden seat is not inviting, but when properly shaped it becomes easy. And there is no objection to a cushion, used of old more commonly even than now. A cushion is more sanitary than upholstery, as a cushion admits of beating and airing.

The WINDSOR is the lightest of chairs, considering its durability. It is easily moved. And it is low in cost — at least, when new.

The common kitchen chair is really a WINDSOR reduced to its lowest terms. The Concord wagon seat, so common in the last generation, had a true WINDSOR back.

The final merit of the WINDSOR is its beauty. Though its lines are so simple, it is at its best very dignified, attractive, and decorative. Indeed, so far have admirers of it gone that they place it in a parlor. It really is appropriate in some form in almost any room except the parlor, in an eighteenth or nineteenth century house.

English Double-back Arm WINDSOR

Condition: Fine and original.

Merit: The English WINDSORS lack grace. Observe how stubby and shapeless the arms are. The bow is very heavy without being stronger for its purpose than a lighter one. The splat is peculiar to the English type.

In fact the spindles in the English chair were added to increase the comfort of the sitter and enhance the "sack back" effect. The American saw no reason for not making all spindles with no splat.

The legs are a very poor feature in English WINDSORS. They are too nearly vertical and start too near the corner of the seat for strength or beauty, and their turnings are very clumsy.

Date: Early type, though continued in England to a middle or even late period.

Occurrence: Very common in England.

Owned by WALLACE NUTTING, Cutler-Bartlet House, 32 Green Street, Newburyport, Mass.

Short Arm, Heavy Rail Bow-back

Condition: The bow is restored, and also the feet behind.

Merit: Very high. The shape of the arms is fine, both as to their sharp outward turn, or ramp, and the carved knuckle. But both are rather heavy. The turnings are the Pennsylvania type with ball ends, and are not so graceful as the northern type.

The seat is perfect, being saddle-shaped, not only as seen in the picture, but, as looked down upon, the front edge is also "scrolled," or cut in a double saddle curve from the center each way.

Owing to the sharp incut or "ramp," at the sides of the seat, the front arm spindles must slant sharply to keep behind the incut.

It is easy to see in the heavy arm rail of this chair how closely it resembles a roundabout chair rail.

Date: Very early.

Occurrence: Very rare.

Owned by WALLACE NUTTING, Hazen Garrison House, 8 Groveland Street, Haverhill, Mass.

The Heavy Rail

The arms in the heavy type of WINDSOR chair are continuous with a level semi-circular back rail which is reinforced in the back by a second piece placed over the joint of the two parts, to unite or splice them. In the chair opposite this work is so nicely done that no joint appears. A handsome molding ends the center splice on each arm — a kind of step-down.

High Bow-back, Light Arm

Condition: Good; apparently original.

Merit: Very high. This chair is very simple and belongs to the lighter type of bow-backs. The special merit is the great height of thè back above the seat. It thus answered as a head rest, a rare thing in a plain bow-back, but common enough in comb-backs. It is surprising that not more chairs of this sort were made; for by their great rarity we judge they were always relatively scarce. There is a pleasing enlargement of the bow just before its tenon enters the rail. The chair is a notable example of the grace obtained through sheer simplicity.

Yet it fails in some particulars. It should have been planned to have nine long spindles, and thus arrange the side spindles nearer together and afford a gradual fan space, avoiding in part the present uneven spacing.

The turnings are good, but not so deep as the best. The turned arm spindles match the legs.

Date: Early, but we cannot assign it the earliest date, as the chair shows progress through a period of refinement to a light type.

Occurrence: Extremely rare. It is almost impossible to discover such chairs out of collections. The writer has not seen one on sale for several years. The comb-backs are much sought, but this chair is still more a "find."

Owned by the Metropolitan Museum, Bowles Collection.

Nine-spindle, Comb-back Windsor

Condition: Fine and apparently original.

Merit: Very high. The comb is fine, with nine spindles, the ideal number in this type. The legs are turned in the early Pennsylvania style, and the middle stretcher is good. The arms are simply scrolled on the outside.

Date: Early.

Occurrence: Rare.

Owned by ARTHUR LESLIE GREEN, Weaver House, Newport, R. I.

The Ideal Windsor Arm Chair

The writer has never seen it. In a settee the best ten legger in this book fairly reaches the mark of an ideal. The earliest type of bow (otherwise round or hoop) back side chair shown is also ideal. Some of the fan-backs also leave little to be desired. But the ideal Windsor Arm Chair should have:

1. Beautiful, heavy, deep-cut vase-turned legs with stretchers of a bold, heavy character in the bulb, and with a good rake to the legs.

2. A finely saddled seat, of large size.

3. Arms with fine, sharp ramp and with large, well-carved knuckles.

4. A nine-spindle comb running up through a double bow and crowned by a finely shaped rail with nicely spiraled carved ears.

Nine-spindle, Comb-back WINDSOR

Condition: Five long spindles had to be renewed; the sides of the feet were mended where rockers had been, but legs were not spliced, being of original length.

Merit: Very high. The chair is large, dignified, and finely symmetrical. The comb is high, and ears are exceptionally fine. The seat is very good; the turnings of the feet terminate like those of the love seat shown.

The "blunt arrow" style.

Date: Early, Pennsylvanian.

Occurrence: Rare of this size and symmetry.

Owned by WALLACE NUTTING, Cutler-Bartlet House, Newburyport, Mass.

A notable feature of this chair is that the front legs are set in five inches from the side of the seat, which is more than twenty-five inches wide.

Comparing the chair opposite with that on the previous page, this chair is somewhat larger. The shaping of the arms here is the same but wider. Both are chairs of much dignity. Notice that the spindles here are not set so near the edge of the seat. This is a merit as it adds to strength. Both chairs have their legs well and properly set in on the seat. In the previous chair, however, they do not completely pierce the seat. Both methods were followed. It was simpler to run the leg away through the seat.

Braced-back, One-piece Back and Arm

Condition: Very fine and original.

Merit: The highest, because it lacks no feature whatever, of its style. Practically perfect in its period (except as to its seven spindles), in arms, seat, splay, style, and almost perfect in the leg turnings. If the smallest part of turning in the vase had been slightly smaller, we could see no way of improvement. An earlier chair would have heavier bulbs.

Date: Early.

Occurrence: Very rare in a form so perfect.

Owned by WALLACE NUTTING, Cutler-Bartlet House, Newburyport, Mass.

This chair, like all of its style, is open to the objection that the arm almost always breaks at the sharp bend. Yet the type is graceful and light. Of course the arm is not so handsome as the knuckle arm, and this style the writer has never seen with a knuckle.

It will be noticed that chairs with brace backs are not so likely as plain-backed chairs to have nine plain spindles, because the two raked bracing spindles require space. The ideal chair would have eight or nine spindles and the braces, like some in this book.

The Comb-back Chair

This variety is more eagerly sought than any other, because it combines many lines of beauty, and by the fireside it speaks much of "old forgotten far off things." We may be sure that its great height of back was used to drape a shawl to serve as a protection against draught, and that it succeeded the clumsy settle, which was difficult to move, and always in the way. The literature of the home will not be complete until a proper tale is written centering around a comb-back chair.

Bow-back, Knuckle-arm WINDSOR

Condition: Good and apparently original.

Merit: Moderate. This type is good, the weight is slight, and so easily moved. The turnings are good but not fine; the knuckles and the spindles well shaped. The seat, as often in this type, is too shallow from front to back, as if for use at a dining table. The seat lacks a chamfer on the under side and so appears heavy, and the spindles are too few.

Date: Early.

Owned (but not on view) *by* WALLACE NUTTING, Framingham, Mass.

Chairs of this style are very common without the knuckle and are the lightest of the arm chairs, as well as the strongest for their weight. This is probably what the old inventories refer to as the "sack-backt" chair.

The spindles were not in the early period turned in a lathe, but were shaved in a vise or whittled by holding in the hand and working each way. Hence was naturally developed the bulb in the spindles, so marked in this example. The bulb necessarily came below the middle as a long, slender taper was required above, to slide through the arm rail. The type once established was then used for side chairs.

The knuckle was almost always formed by glueing a piece to the under side of the rail. This method was more economical of wood than to work the knuckle out of the solid.

In this particular chair the arm rail is bent and therefore small· It requires, to be in good taste, small knuckles, such as on page 24. The dainty little knuckles are wonderfully attractive. The arm ends are also sometimes wrought in this type as three open fingers.

Comb-back, Heavy-arm WINDSOR

Condition: Feet pieced.

Merit: High, for general appearance and grace. The back and arms are excellent, but the gap between the long and short spindle is unnecessary, and the under body turnings are not choice. Observe that the knuckle is all cut on the thin arm, and lacks the fullness of the preceding knuckle.

Date: Early to middle period.

Occurrence: Unusual.

Owned by WALLACE NUTTING, 32 Green Street, Newburyport, Mass.

Footstools

The WINDSOR type, or "stick leg," was well adapted for footstools. The earliest simple stools in America apparently had a boot-jack end leg made in one piece. But with the WINDSOR style came the stool, which was either round topped or oval, with a thinned edge to give a light effect. Footstools were in very common use partly as convenient seats for children, but principally because the floors were so cold that as soon as one sat down a stool was the first thought. The cellars were cold of necessity, to preserve the winter's food.

Little opening for artistic designing was afforded in the short-legged stool, but one of a real udder shape is highly amusing. The cow's udder was the obvious model, and with reason, for the legs got thickness of wood where they needed it and the stool was elsewhere lightened.

Bow-back Arm Windsor

Condition: Fine and apparently original.

Merit: Very high for its type. The turnings are very good; possibly not so massive as the very earliest, but closely approaching them. The stretchers are the earliest sort. The knuckle is very handsomely carved. The seat is 18¼ inches high in front. The back 44¼ inches high.

Peculiar in the feature of stopping the arms on the bow and having no arm rail to run around the chair. This of course adds to comfort by affording the long spring of the back spindles as in the side chair. The feature is shown in several instances in this book on fan-back arm chairs, but this is a rare feature in the bow back with arm and no arm rail. The method of construction, however, is not secure. The junction of bow and arm must be weak unless as elsewhere in this book the bow is enlarged to receive the arm. One also feels that nine back spindles instead of seven would materially enhance the chair's merit, for in that case the spindles could have been a little lighter. The arms also lack the grace of a ramp, and are almost straight.

Date: Early.

Occurrence: Extremely rare.

Owned by Clement C. Littlefield, Newfields, N. H.

Light Comb-back

Condition: Fine and original.

Merit: Moderate.   The turnings of underbody are good; also those of front spindles; there are lightly carved arms.   The comb is not very good.   Seat good.

Date: Early to middle period.

Occurrence: Of only moderate rarity.

Owned by WALLACE NUTTING, 32 Green St., Newbury-port, Mass.

The object of a light arm, all the knuckles being made of one piece, was to lighten the whole chair.   WINDSORS derive one of their merits from their easy portability.   This chair was evidently designed by one who lacked time or skill or taste to form a spiral ear, or to give the spindles a nice contour.   The spindles of this date begin to be turned rather than cut by hand.   The back rest of the lathe, an invention made about this time, rendered turning of small spindles possible.   But the process of turning a small long spindle is very long and expensive.   Hence even after the back rest of the lathe came into use the spindles were not always turned.   In chairs of this type the arm rail is bent of hickory or white oak.

It is clear from such chairs as this that the maker sometimes forgot the obligation to make a thing beautiful, and kept himself to sheer utility so far as the comb is concerned.   We must admit that a long-eared comb was an additional thing to run against. But once seen a good comb is not to be dispensed with.   We incline to the notably true sentiment that we can get on without necessities, but not without luxuries!   It would be interesting to know how the curved and lengthened ear happened to be developed.   Is it possible it was found a convenient hook on which to hang a "Betty lamp"?   The writer finds such a lamp will give just the right light so hung, while hung *inside* the ear, as would be necessary here, it would be too much behind one.

Open-hand Scroll Arm Bow-back

Condition: Two of the legs are new; the other two are pieced.

Merit: Moderate. All the features are very good, but not the best. It would seem that makers were afraid to cut deeply in turning, for fear of weakening the leg. The obvious answer is that they could have made the bulbs larger, thus securing the same relative values. The nine long spindles are well placed, and sprung to fan shape.

Date: Early.

Occurrence of the open hand carving on arm is rare.

Owned by WALLACE NUTTING, 32 Green Street, Newburyport, Mass.

In this chair the spindles are turned, and are too heavy. Perhaps they were made before the lathe rest came in, and could only be turned heavily. The more spindles in a chair the more it gets a cozy, closed-in appearance and the more comfortable the back is. This chair seat assumes a nearly true oval. In case a ramp or curved side incut is made in the seat, in front of the last spindle, the spindles are crowded back at the bottom and slant forward more at the top, thus producing the "short arm" WINDSOR.

When the seat is quite shallow the chair admits of being brought closer to a table. Yet it is more of a support than a seat and would indicate that the occupant was not supposed to linger long at table. In such a chair "fifteen minutes are enough" as a notable authority has said regarding the time of all meals but dinner. The arms were designed to slip just under the edge of the table.

Low-back Arm WINDSOR

Condition: Fine and apparently original.

Merit: High for the type. The seat is especially well shaped and the chair is large. The legs are of the Pennsylvania sort, and while inferior to the Northern turning are the best the writer has seen of their kind. The blunt arrow termination is especially good. We could wish that the arm had been carved, but this seems not to have been done in chairs of this kind. The back is peculiar and suggests the possible origin of the modern office chair. The height of this piece is remarkable and of course adds to the ease of the chair.

Date: Middle period.

Occurrence: Very rare.

Owned by E. R. LEMON, Wayside Inn, So. Sudbury, Mass.

Material of WINDSORS

A WINDSOR chair is composed of several kinds of wood. The merit consists not in the kind of wood, but in its shape. The obvious reason for using pine for the seat is that it was very easily worked and neither warped, swelled, or shrunk so much as other woods. The seat should always be in one piece, and never glued up of two parts. The legs and stretchers are usually maple; the bow (or hoop), the top-rail, and spindles were hickory, white oak, or ash. The arm-rail was maple when heavy and sawed; when light and bent it was of the same wood as the bow. The comb was hickory or oak, and rarely ash, which is not so good as it splinters too readily.

Bow-back Arm Windsor

Condition: Fine and original.

Merit: Moderate. The bow is high enough to be rather more graceful than most bow-back chairs, and the seven long spindles have a fine fan-curve. The turnings are fairly good. One could wish the maker had planned nine spindles instead of seven to run to the bow. It would have added much grace, and avoided the lack of corelation where the first short spindle stops. A common omission.

Date: Middle period.

Occurrence: Common except for the finely sprung spindles.

Owned by Wallace Nutting, Cutler-Bartlet House, 32 Green St., Newburyport, Mass.

Marks of Age

The earlier chairs never have the long, light spindles turned. Examination shows that every spindle is shaped by hand, though perhaps polished in a lathe. Therefore many a fine chair shows variation in the size (though not in the style) of the spindles.

These long, light spindles in early chairs never have any ornament, except one slight bulb. They could not be made with two or more bulbs, therefore bamboo-shaped spindles are always found on later chairs.

Recent investigation shows that even the lathe rest will not make possible the turning of the lightest and longest spindles. Hence in modern reproductions they are never seen. A lathe with a ring rest, however, is capable of making the longest and lightest work, but in modern factories it is "too much trouble" or expense to use it.

31

Heavy-rail, Nine-spindle Comb-back

Condition: The stretchers, while very old, are not original. One front spindle is new, and one long spindle.

Merit: High. The proportions are fine, but the ears are not so good as the carved type. The style of the legs is the ball termination. A large, high chair of much dignity.

Date: Early.

Occurrence: Unusual.

Owned by WALLACE NUTTING, Wentworth-Gardner House, Portsmouth, N. H.

————

Painting

A brightly shining WINDSOR is offensive. The early finish was often the old Indian red. This was more a stain than a paint. A modern substitute for it, under that name, is obtainable.

The old Indian red was used on panel work, chests, settles, and chairs with great impartiality and generous abandon. It is not bright and supplies a good finish today.

Red paint is also a popular old finish. There was not too much color in our ancestors' lives and they loved to make it appear in their furniture.

Dark green seems to have been the most popular color and most satisfactory. WINDSORS are in old advertisements often mentioned as green. It is a very desirable color. But light green is perhaps the worst of all, except white.

Heavy, Nine-spindle Comb-back
WINDSOR

Condition: Now fine, but the seat has been filled and the feet restored.

Merit: Moderate. A slight spring in the long spindles is graceful. A very large chair, of origin south of New England. The legs lack sufficient rake. The bottoms are in the right place but the tops should have been set in a little. The arms are plain. The style of the legs and stretcher is unusual and not especially meritorious. Somewhat lacking in grace.

Peculiar in the buttons at the centers of the very fine ears. These buttons are raised, an effect obtained by turning separately and inserting them on a stem or post in a hole which goes through the comb.

Date: Middle period.

Occurrence: Unusual, buttons extremely so.

Owned by WALLACE NUTTING, Webb-Washington House, 89 Main Street, Wethersfield, Conn.

The Finish of the WINDSOR

The natural wood, a handsome finish, was unusual, but examples are known. There is no objection to it, surely, in refinishing an old chair that must be refinished, for the wood color is very homelike. But the patience and expense required to clean an old WINDSOR are great, and often are more than the piece is worth. The mechanic may say what he will, but no kind of paint remover will work without assistance by the elbow. In the fine creases of the turnings and elsewhere carelessness is damaging. A brush should be used for cleaning.

Comb-back Arm WINDSOR

Condition: Fine.

Merit: Very high. Comparing it with the following chair
the seat is finer, having the side ramp. In other respects it is an even thing between them. The legs
could be somewhat better as in the following example.
It will be seen that owing to the shape of the seat the
front arm was set on a sharp rake, in pleasing contrast
to the leg below.

Date: Early.

Occurrence: Very rare.

Owned by the METROPOLITAN MUSEUM, New York.

Warning

"Photographic accuracy" is a term used only by persons who
do not understand a lens, which by nature always exaggerates, and
when the object pictured is near the disproportionate enlargement
of the foreground is very great. As a consequence, in this and all
other furniture books, the seats and front parts of a chair are shown
much too large relatively, and there is no way of avoiding this
result. The student should, therefore, remember to imagine the
comb backs larger than they are shown. A chair pictured from the
rear appears to be nearly all back.

Style

An important matter of style is the rake of the legs, otherwise
called splay or slant. A WINDSOR without this rake is graceless. No
other type of chair has splayed legs, because in the WINDSOR
only does the leg go into a hole in the seat. The bulbs in the side
stretchers were no doubt formed to give greater strength at the
junction with the cross stretcher, but the cross stretcher itself was
then supplied with a bulb because its shape was discovered to be
graceful, and was probably first made bulbous through the accident of using an extra side stretcher for the cross stretcher.

Comb-back, Heavy-Arm **Windsor**

Condition: Original, except for pieced feet and seat.

Merit: High. Were the legs a little better, the chair would stand in the highest class possible, as most of the other features are very fine indeed. The seat is above twenty-one inches wide. The arm chairs have a height from seat to rail of nine to ten inches.

Date: Early.

Occurrence: Rare with so many good features.

Owned by **Wallace Nutting**, Wentworth-Gardner House, Portsmouth, N. H.

————

The Comb

It is shaped by steaming and clamping to a form to give it the proper concavity, and the more the better. After it has become set it is finished and adjusted to its place on the spindles. But it appears that some old combs did not get or keep the proper curvature. Nothing adds so much to a chair for so little trouble as a finely curved, delicately scrolled back. The upper edge should be thinned almost to a knife edge. No wood is left in a **Windsor** except strength requires it.

The comb is otherwise called the top rail, to distinguish it from the lower or arm rail. Its thickness, where the spindles enter it, is often not more than a half inch, and never in good chairs more than five eighths of an inch. It was, therefore, a delicate piece of joinery to bore the holes for the spindles. It is clear why the toughest woods like hickory were used for the rail.

Taste differs in choosing between a somewhat heavy and rugged comb and a comb quite narrow. Of course the comb must keep its strength by avoiding the cutting of deep holes for spindles.

39

Triple-back Arm WINDSOR

Condition: The fourth, that is the top back, is a later
addition as appears by the great inequality in the
spacing of its spindles, not seen in the rest of the chair;
by the fact that these spindles are not a continuation
of the long spindles of the chair; and by the fact that
the third back, that is the one under the added back,
has a scroll top and was therefore clearly the original
top of the chair, the fourth back being coarser and out
of harmony. This fourth back makes the chair top
heavy, especially as the feet were cut down to add the
rockers.

Merit: Nevertheless high as it combines the round and
comb-backs, has nine spindles in the proper comb; has
carved "open hand" arms. The turnings are poor.

Date: Middle period.

Occurrence: Very rare.

Owned by GEORGE PLYMPTON, Walpole, Mass.

One could wish to see this chair restored to its original condition
by removing the fourth back and piecing the feet. It is so rare
that all its merits ought to be preserved. The object of the very
long original comb was to give something like a wing-chair shape,
but the extension of the comb sidewise is not graceful, supported
as it is by extra, inharmonious spindles.

Colors of WINDSORS

Black, not so common originally, is a most excellent finish, for it
not only covers a multitude of sins, but is harmonious with any
other furniture. As there are no heavy, broad lines in WINDSORS,
black is not somber, and will be found the most satisfactory of all
for modern finish.

Yellow was not uncommon, especially in children's chairs.

Brown and even drab are found. But white should be avoided.
Not a good word can be said for it. It is bad taste through and
through. The fad for it, to match chamber furniture, is inexcusable.

Double Comb-back WINDSOR

Condition: Fine and original, unless the little ears are later carving, which is probable. The upholstery is, of course, an addition.

Merit: Very high. The treatment is dainty in the back, and very suggestive of what WINDSORS are capable of being made. For instance, a nine-spindle back could have carried the upper comb on five spindles. Turnings are only fair, except stretchers, which are very good. Another peculiarity of this chair is a pleasing vertical concavity of the back, such that it is even more attractive sidewise than in front.

Date: Early to middle period.

Occurrence: Extremely rare.

Owned by ARTHUR LESLIE GREEN, Weaver House, Newport, R. I.

Best Colors

To give in another form a color scheme, one would do well to use green for porch and country house use; black for dining room or living room; yellow for the nursery or simple chambers, and natural finish anywhere. A heavy layer of paint, on an otherwise fine chair, sometimes obliterates its fine lines. It is best to clean carefully, when two coats well rubbed down produce a very fine effect.

Triple-Back WINDSOR

Condition: Fair; feet pieced.

Merit: High. One comb rising above the double back is a feature of marked merit, although it is not well shaped. The spindles and stretchers are fine, legs poor and should have been tapered more in their restoration.

Date: Early middle period.

Occurrence: Extremely rare owing to the triple back.

Owned by the CITY OF NEW YORK in the Old City Hall.

The maker of this chair started with a good idea, but failed to carry it out. Probably there is somewhere a chair with a better comb and turnings of a higher character.

The Joinery of WINDSORS

While the cabinet maker disdains a WINDSOR, a very large degree of skill was required to make a chair which had style and would retain its solidity. Like other turned chairs, its legs were sometimes made of green wood. The stretchers were dry. The end of the stretcher to be driven into the leg was formed with a hollowed groove. Thus when it was driven home, and the green leg shrank around the bulb, a joint was formed that could not be separated without breaking the wood. Thus a well-made WINDSOR, though light, was far more rigid than the Jacobean chairs which, however handsome, have mostly broken, and those that remain incline to be treacherously weak.

45

Comb-back WINDSOR

Condition: Legs are cut short.

Merit: High. The turnings and the seat are good, and the simply scrolled arm has a good outward ramp. But the peculiar merit of the chair is the very gracefully set back. The comb is deeply concaved, nearly a half circle, a feature difficult to show in a photograph. The spindle effect is very good. The back legs are set too near the front legs.

Date: Early.

Occurrence: Very rare, with a back as good.

Owned by WALLACE NUTTING, 32 Green Street, Newburyport, Mass.

If the WINDSOR seat was green it shrunk with the green leg, but this point was the one place in the chair where green and dry could not be matched together.

The spindles, of course, were dry. This made them rigid when green seat and bow shrunk around them; and a well-made chair was like one solid, airy shape of wood, so well done that many are without a loose joint today, after the use and abuse of four or five generations.

The leg, where it did not completely penetrate the seat, was sometimes rendered secure in this manner: A hole was bored, increasing in size with the depth. A fox-tail wedge was merely started and as the leg was driven home the wedge penetrated and spread the end to conform with the hole.

Comb-back, Short-arm Windsor

Condition: Fine and apparently original.

Merit: High, owing to the remarkable grace and good taste in which one part falls in with another. The comb is especially good, with finely out-sprung spindles, seven in number, all that a chair of this small sort can have in the comb. The arm suggests the English, and is plain. The size is moderate — perhaps a "lady" chair. The leg turnings are fair; not deep enough; but the stretchers are satisfactory. The seat is graceful.

Date: Uncertain, but early or middle period.

Occurrence: Rare.

Owned by Arthur Leslie Green, Weaver House, Newport, R. I.

The Windsor Seat

The saddle of the early chairs always drooped away from the center all the way to the side, and was obviously designed for a male occupant to sprawl in. The later chair had a not ungraceful seat with a curve dropping away from the saddle and rising again at the sides. The above remarks apply, of course, to side chairs.

Early arm chairs in which spindles were set all the way around to the front, settee fashion, could not, of course, be cut away saddle fashion at the sides. Where the arm was short, or the front spindles were back of the side ramp, the seat preserved even in arm chairs its primitive shape. At the back and the sides so far as the spindles continued the seat was left full thickness. But as soon as the spindles ceased at the sides and in front the seat was chamfered away on the under side in a long slant to give the effect of lightness, and in fine specimens the chamfer of the saddle above meets that underneath, in a feather edge.

49

Comb-back, Short-arm WINDSOR

Condition: Fine and apparently original.

Merit: Moderate. Turnings odd. Comb good and unusually large for the chair.

Date: Middle period.

Occurrence: Rare.

Owned by ARTHUR LESLIE GREEN, Weaver House, Newport, R. I.

One will do well to compare the three pictures last given. All
show chairs of similar design yet each with merits of its own. The
one on page 46 has the poorest base but the finest top — in fact
an ideal top of this sort. That on page 48 shows the best seat and
best-shaped spindles. On this page the chair has not the graceful
top of either of the others, yet it is rarely flaring and interesting.

———

The Height of the Seat

Eighteen inches from the top of the seat, at the highest point of
the saddle in a vertical line to the floor, is good style. This height
corresponded with the height of late Jacobean and Pilgrim chairs
which the WINDSOR supplanted, from 1725 to 1750. The height was
gradually cut almost to seventeen inches. In measuring about a
thousand old WINDSORS only one was found under seventeen inches
without evidences that the legs were cut down.

Since this handbook was begun the writer has obtained a side
chair, not cut down, and yet only fourteen inches and a fraction,
in height. It has blunt arrow turnings, a fine rake of the legs, and
is admirably fitted for a small person.

Braced-back, Bow, Mahogany-arm
WINDSOR

Condition: Fine; slight cut on feet.

Merit: High. The seat is excellent and of the early type. The turnings, however, of the spindles are done in a lathe and not by hand. Turnings of legs good, not the best.

Date: Middle period.

Occurrence: Unusual in so good a form.

Owned by WALLACE NUTTING, Cutler-Bartlet House, Newburyport, Mass.

This chair never appears in the generous bigness of the great old comb-backs, but is very convenient for moving about. It shows the refinement of fanciful turnings in the spindles, which never appears in early examples. This type of concaved turning below the vase is said to indicate a Rhode Island origin, but the good effect is here lost by the cutting off of the feet.

It is a curious question how the spindles of this chair were turned as the outside ones in the back were pipe stems. They could only have been done by a patient person who was willing to support his work by at least two back rests. The brace spindles are too small to be of much use. Yet there is so much springiness of the back that it has held firmly together. The attachment of the arms to the bow in this style is not structurally good, there being no manner of holding the end wood securely.

Round-back Arm Chair with Comb

Condition: Rockers not original. Seat strengthened by battens; one arm restored.

Merit: Chiefly in its peculiarities. The arms carry a continuation of the bead on the bow. The comb is arched, and nearly follows the line of the bow back. The spindles are brought down to a small diameter below the swell. Turnings, bamboo style.

Date: Late.

Occurrence: Rare, as regards the shape of arms and bow.

Owned by Arthur Leslie Green, Newport, R. I.

Chairs having a comb above a bow like the above are popularly sought. The rockers seem not to be an objection to many collectors. But the tendency is now away from rockers. No original rocker appears in this book.

———

Pitfalls for the Novice

Windsors have been little studied and even the dealers may honestly recommend as good what is not so. But it is noticeable that no good arm chair remains long on sale if the price is at all reasonable. One should look very carefully to learn if the piece is too low, or if the feet are pieced. Also whether the arm, especially in the one-piece-bow-and-arm, is not split or mended. Every spindle should be tested top and bottom. Beware of new paint. It covers something that detracts from value. See if the stretchers agree in style; also the spindles. A haggled chair may have value. Some dealers, especially those remote from centers, are not cognizant of good points and will sell at low prices, but it is hardly safe to presume on the ignorance of a dealer.

Comb-back, no Outside Spindles

Condition: Apparently original.

Merit: Moderate, but the chair is very interesting because it shows a memory of the English style of arm. The maker, however, adopted the conventional American scroll on the outside of the arm and the rest of the chair is American. It, of course, needs more spindles.

Date: Early to middle period.

Occurrence: In this odd form very rare.

Owned by MRS. ANNIE B. HUNTER, Freehold, N. J.

Oddities

The author has shown no chair with the cabriole leg because it does not come under the proper definition of WINDSOR. The cabriole leg appeared so freely in Dutch and Chippendale furniture and in such perfection that it appears a misfortune to place a depraved form of it on a WINDSOR chair, while an elegant form would clearly spoil the rest of the chair. Thus also WINDSORS are found with pommel feet, that is, a knob termination projecting in front of the true line of the leg. This is not ungraceful, but it cannot be turned, and is clearly an adaption from the Lancaster (English) foot.

All such oddities have an interest, and perhaps that interest is greater than it should be. A mere oddity has a commercial but not an artistic value. A departure from style is agreeable; not a departure from good taste.

Braced, Fan-back Arm WINDSOR

Condition: Fine and original.

Merit: Very high, and the highest of its type. The seat is wide, the carving and out-curve of the arms fine. One could wish two or three more spindles had been added in the back. The bracing spindles, if set a little nearer together at the top, would have allowed more regular spindles. It has back side spindles of very large size, increasing all the way to the seat, and affording strength, but somewhat suggestive of the need of a larger lower body. The tongue which supports the two raking and bracing spindles is mortised into the seat, instead of being as usual of the same piece of wood. This is logical and necessary across the grain.

Date: Early to middle period.

Occurrence: Rare.

Owned by WILLIAM F. HUBBARD, Hartford, Conn. The writer also owns, at the Webb House, Wethersfield, a chair very similar.

Mahogany Arms

This feature indicates a middle to late period, and the arm always scrolls up and down, modern fashion, rather than outward. Obviously the mahogany arm was designed to contrast in color with the rest of the chair, which could not, therefore, have been finished in natural color.

Fan-back Arm WINDSOR

Condition: Feet pieced; otherwise original.

Merit: Very high.   Leg turning only fair; back outside spindles fine.

Peculiar in the rather graceless straightness of the arms, in spite of their carving.   But peculiarly meritorious in the handsome squaring of the outside back spindles.

Date: Middle period.

Occurrence: Rare.

Owned by WALLACE NUTTING, Cutler-Bartlet House, 32 Green St., Newburyport, Mass.

Rockers

We have heard of original WINDSOR rockers, but, possibly with one exception, have not seen them.   Elsewhere remarks are made as to the means of knowing that rockers are not original.   As it is no longer good form to rock and for that matter never could have been, we need not grieve over the false WINDSOR rocker, except to regret that so many thousand perfectly good WINDSORS have been spoiled by adding rockers.

In modern WINDSORS rockers usually omit the stretchers which form a clumsy combination with the rocker.

Undoubtedly the "Boston rocker," was the most popular chair for common use.   The spindles were made on a lathe with a ring and follower, or a back gauge.

Short-arm, Fan-back WINDSOR

Condition: The balls of the feet are partly worn off, and the middle stretcher is not original, lacking the bulb. Otherwise very good.

Merit: High because of its peculiarities, and its transitional type from the English WINDSOR. It suffers from a very heavy seat.

Peculiar in the remarkable middle spindle which has two sharply marked bulbs, the lower one probably being designed to make the sitter keep an upright position. The chair shows ideas of grace which in this spindle perhaps forgot the idea of comfort. The spindle suggests that the maker had in his mind a reminiscence of the splat in English WINDSORS. The outside back spindles are very graceful and have a very rare turned (instead of squared) enlargement to receive the arms.

Date: Early, Pennsylvanian with English influence?

Occurrence: Perhaps unique.

Owned by ARTHUR LESLIE GREEN, Weaver House, Newport, R. I.

The "Boston rocker" is the middle of last-century degradation of the WINDSOR. It was and is even now extremely common. But the machine-made seat lacked reason and the rail was bold and graceless. It was a purely commercial article, made to sell at a low price.

Short-arm, Fan-back WINDSOR

Condition: Good, but rockers are not original, and connection between arms and outside back spindles is not so secure as it should be owing to lack of size in those spindles.

Merit: Moderate. The seat is almost round front and back. The arms have a pleasant rapid outward sweep, rather away from a sitter. The chair is small; turnings poor.

Date: Middle to late period.

Occurrence: Unusual.

Owned by WALLACE NUTTING, Cutler-Bartlet House, 32 Green Street, Newburyport, Mass.

The " Slipper " Chair

The so-called "slipper" chair, which many dealers have a way of slipping off on their customers, had an existence, as the writer owns one. The fact that there was such a chair has merely given an excuse for pretending that the particular WINDSOR on sale has not been cut down.

Nor will it answer to maintain that the legs have worn off. Not much more than a half of an inch can be allowed for such wear, for maple is hard and WINDSORS have not existed for centuries.

Bow-back WINDSOR with Arms

Condition: Perfect and original.

Merit: High. A thoroughly consistent double-joint bamboo-turned bow-back, with delicate mahogany arms. Note the change in this from an arm curving *sidewise* to one curving *up and down*, the direction of the curves being changed as soon as the mahogany arm appears. This chair is remarkable for its wide seat and wider base, and has nine spindles. It came down in the Willard family of clock makers. Color red.

Date: Latish.

Occurrence: Rare in a shape so good.

Owned by WALLACE NUTTING, Cutler-Bartlet House, Newburyport, Mass.

Where WINDSORS are Found

New England is now the only district where WINDSORS are not very rare. A few, better or worse, can often be found in New England dealers' hands, and they are still quite general in many households, and are in present-day use, and far more difficult to buy from homes than from shops.

Their values have doubled in three or four years, and multiplied many times in twenty years. A fine WINDSOR settee is rarer than a Chippendale settee.

Kinked, Bow-back Arm WINDSOR

Condition: Fine and original.

Merit: This chair has as meritorious points nine spindles
in the back; the arms and outside arm spindles of
mahogany are handsomely adjusted so as to suggest a
double Flemish curve. The seat is fairly good and the
bamboo turnings show two joints throughout.

Peculiar in the kink of the bow some inches above the
seat. This oddity may or may not be counted a merit.

Date: Late.

Occurrence: Unusual.

Owned by WALLACE NUTTING, Cutler-Bartlet House, Newburyport, Mass.

A List of Terms Connected with the Seat

Incut or ramp. The concave curve at the side of the seat just in
front of the arms.

Saddle. The shaping of the seat by which it is left full thickness
at the center, in front, and is either hollowed on each side, in the
middle period, or falls away to the outer edge in the early period.

Tailpiece or brace or extension back. The piece extending from
the back of the seat to receive the two slanting spindles on a braced-
back chair.

Chamfer. The cutting away of the edge of the seat above or
below.

Comb-back WINDSOR

Condition: Strong, but a botch.

Merit: An amazing instance of how not to do it. The chair has been "converted" into a rocker, and that not righteously but wickedly. It is shown as a curious example of haggling, supposedly to catch a customer.

The first oddity is the location of the stretchers, running into the vase rather than below into the plain taper, where they always occur. In this chair trouble was taken to remove them from their original position, to make room for the rockers. These rockers have each a hole plugged in the center apparently with the idea of a stretcher, which was later abandoned. The chair is large, with scrolled, not carved, arms. Had it been left in its original form the chair would have been highly meritorious, but there is a persistent demand, or was, for rockers. The middle stretcher and front spindles look too good and too new to be true. The chair was obtained from one of the most notorious fakers of antiques.

Date: Parts are early.

Owned (as a horrible example) *by* WALLACE NUTTING, Framingham, Mass.

After all we can say derogatory of such a chair, the scheme of its underbody is the best that could be devised for a WINDSOR with both rockers and stretchers. Sad to say, it is being widely copied to-day. ¡The comb is one of the best ever seen, being not only very much concaved but very long.

71

" Duck-bill " Joint, Turned-back Windsor

Condition: Fine and original.

Merit: High for its period. While the legs show the plain late style the whole effect is excellent. It is the sort of chair that anyone likes. The writer has invented the name given above, and it may not be of any value, but it at least calls attention to the *peculiar* feature. The joint of the outer spindles with the horizontal piece, while done by mortise and tenon, outwardly looks like a dainty prolonged miter, like a duck bill.

Date: Very late.

Occurrence: Rare.

Owned by William F. Hubbard, Hartford, Conn.

The style above is being commonly reproduced, though without the fine points of the "duck bill." Its simplicity is a recommendation. Its seat can be easily shaped by machinery. Carried out in the style of the seat and turnings on page 66 it would become more attractive, but all these improvements would entail an expense better indulged in an earlier and more meritorious type. The base of most Windsors is much greater than the width of the seat. In this respect they are a wide departure from the Jacobean, which insisted on vertical lines, and was always top heavy and liable to overset.

Nomenclature and Origin

The term loop back has been used of a side chair made with a back bow — that is, a round back or hoop ; while the upper bow of the double back — that is, a bow running down to the arm rail — is termed a hoop back. This variance in terms seems to the writer a distinction without a difference. One is as much a loop or a hoop as the other.

The settee-shaped seat also of armchairs, made without a side concavity, has been called the low-back seat. But as the Pennsylvania comb back is far more frequent than the low back, and as both have this sort of seat, it is confusing and questionable to name the seat after the low back merely because that back was earlier. This seat, either straight front or with a soft ogee from the saddle, was the type for all great chairs and settees, and these had also vertical arm supports.

Bow-back Arm WINDSOR

Condition: Feet pieced.

Merit of this chair is mostly in the fine height of the back. In other respects it is not worth dwelling upon. It suggests in its arms the beginning of the Boston rocker of the Victorian period, and shows how much one may unconsciously fall away in taste.

Date: Very late.

Occurrence: Common, except for the bow.

Owned by WALLACE NUTTING, 32 Green Street, Newburyport, Mass.

List of Terms
The Bow

The bow is the horse-shoe or ox-bow shaped piece which forms the outline of the back in bow or "round" back chairs. In ancient chairs it continues curving even into the seat. Later it drew in somewhat before entering seat. In one style it did not enter the seat at all, but in one piece swept down to form the arm — a weak construction.

The Arm

The *arm rail* is the piece which forms both the arm and the lower rail, sweeping round the back from arm to arm. The bow above it, the ends of which fasten into it, is the bow proper. A chair so made is called a sack back. The arm may be plain; merely rounded at the end; or cut on the outside in a scroll; or carved in a spiral like a knuckle, and called a knuckle arm.

"Sheraton" Square-back Arm
WINDSOR

Condition: Fine and apparently original.

Merit: Moderate, though good of its type. It resembles closely in the back the late settees. It also has the merit of nine back spindles, but as in late chairs the seat lacks grace. The arm suggests the ancestry of the "Boston Rocker."

Date: Very late.

Occurrence: Rare.

Owned by WALLACE NUTTING, Cutler-Bartlet House, Newburyport, Mass.

Prices

As to the prices paid, it is of little value to mention them except comparatively. Excellent examples of side chairs are often found for the price of an opera ticket, while two score times as much has doubtless been paid for very fine and rare high-backed arms, or for writing chairs.

Speaking broadly, side chairs in a set are worth twice as much as when found singly. Also the side chair is worth perhaps one-third as much as an arm chair of the same type. Features that increase the price rapidly are very high backs, very large seats, very early dates.

One hundred and fifty dollars is asked in New York for a fine comb back. But if value is to depend on rarity we can of course say nothing certain as to what extent the desire of buyers may rise. Very fair side chairs, singly or in pairs, are as cheap at least as new style mahogany chairs.

Writing-arm WINDSOR

Condition: Fine.   Original except one long spindle.

Merit: The highest.   Observe the quaintly heavy leg on
the table side.   It was made heavier and was raked
more than its mate to take the greater weight and preserve the center of gravity.   It is just such individual
touches as these that give charm to old furniture.
The size of the tongue is huge.   The support of the
table by spindles of the same style as the rest of the
chair is an early and rare feature.   The insprung
spindles of the comb are another quaint feature.   They
are seven.   This is the Sherer chair, always hitherto in
one family, and parted with to the writer merely to
afford the public an opportunity to enjoy it.   The
chair never had drawers.   Turnings could be better.

Date: Very early.

Occurrence: Perhaps unique.

Owned by WALLACE NUTTING, Webb-Washington House,
Wethersfield, Conn.

Rarity of Fine Types

We often hear wonder expressed that fine types of any sort of
furniture are so rare.   The reason is to be found partly in the rarity
of skill, sufficient to have produced them, and again in the rarity of
appreciation that was willing to expend the necessary means for
their production.   But in the case of large pieces such as writing-
arm chairs and ten-legged settees, unless a family was fixed in one
house for many generations such pieces were often counted too
cumbersome to move.

Writing-arm WINDSOR

Condition: Fine and apparently original.

Merit: The highest. The apparent slant to the left of the observer is mostly an optical delusion caused by the intentional slant inward of the table, which is very wide, and therefore the drawer presents a somewhat awkwardly long effect viewed from the front. The turnings are all of the best. A careful study of these turnings will teach a novice for what he should look. For instance, the cut at the bottom of the vase in the legs is very deep and the bulb above it consequently very large. Observe also that the front spindle and table spindles are of the highest merit, better than any others the writer has seen. These turnings usually lack something of style which might easily have been supplied. Note that if one should cut off the leg some inches and taper the portion left he would have a perfect arm spindle, except that, of course it would be a trifle smaller. It is not suggested that the usual arm spindle is not good, but only that this is better, and probably hopeless to look for often. The arm is scrolled and carved. We must admit that the tilting of the table detracts from the grace of the general effect, but is more convenient as it is. The seven-spindle comb could have been better.

Date: Very early.

Occurrence: Extremely rare.

Owned by WALLACE NUTTING, Iron Works House, Saugus Center, Mass.

Light Writing-arm WINDSOR

Condition: Fine and apparently original.

Merit: High. The seat is well shaped and the seven back spindles were intended to be outsprung. Both drawers are correct. The chair is of light weight and rather delicate effect. The legs are somewhat light for the service demanded. The ears are not spiraled but star-carved. It is usual for writing chairs to be made with sawed arm rail. This chair accomplishes much for its weight.

Date: Middle period.

Occurrence: Very rare.

Owned by WALLACE NUTTING, Cutler-Bartlet House, Newburyport, Mass.

The writing-arm chair by its nature cannot be symmetrical. The arm beneath the table is left in the rough, a flat support. Neither is it possible to have the spindles in the comb very numerous or spread far to the side, owing to danger of interference with the writing table. The glorified writing chair has a little slide which may be drawn out as a candle rest. But the writer has never seen a writing chair without some faults.

The writing-arm chair was not made in sufficient numbers to fix a type. Most probably it was made to order and there are no two very nearly alike. The absence of patterns led the maker to work out his problems with more or less success according to his taste. In the example before us he evidently sacrificed to the idea of stability a somewhat wider arm which would have made the chair more serviceable. With a light underbody he could scarcely do better, except that there should have been a greater slant to the two outside spindles that enter the horn and the horn could then have been shorter.

Writing-arm WINDSOR

Condition: Fine.

Merit: Moderate. Has two tongues or supports for the table spindles. Never had drawer under seat. The plain ears, and the five, rather than six or seven, long spindles; the plain arm and ordinary bamboo turnings of the legs (possibly a trifle shortened) keep the chair out of the highest class.

Date: Late middle period.

Occurrence: Writing-arm chairs are rare.

Owned by WALLACE NUTTING, Hospitality Hall, Wethersfield, Conn.

Some writing chairs are made with a swivel arm so as to make it easy to enter or leave the chair, which is a feat otherwise forbidden to very stout men. The swivel arms seem to be late, appearing on chairs which have otherwise lost all good early character. There is much poetry, real and figurative, connected with the writing chair. It is the most inviting of all chairs, because it calls to either work or recreation, and is a little world in itself.

There is at the rooms of the Concord Antiquarian Society a very crude but quaint writing-arm chair which Emerson used for writing some of his essays. The residence of the essayist was opposite and in order to avoid lion-hunters he would sometimes steal away to the Society rooms where he used this chair without molestation. It is made with two boards, the upper one tilted somewhat sloping toward the back and affording a small space between the two boards for paper.

Writing-arm WINDSOR

Condition: Apparently original.

Merit: Moderate owing to its small size and the lack of depth. The suggestion occurs that it may have been designed for a woman. The turnings are bamboo type.

Date: Late middle period.

Occurrence: Rare, as are all writing chairs.

Owned by WILLIAM F. HUBBARD, Hartford, Conn.

The Braced Back

This fine feature consisting of a tailpiece, run out from the seat. Two spindles run slantwise into the bow or rail of the back. The tailpiece when well formed is wedge shaped, narrower where it connects with the chair. In arm chairs, where the grain of the seat runs sidewise, it was necessary to mortise in the tailpiece. But in any other case of framing in one may conclude that the work is a recent fraud. A braced-back chair is strong.

A braced-back chair is worth perhaps a half more than or even twice as much as one without this feature. A chair with a writing arm is the most valuable, except a "three backt" chair (the arm rail, the bow, and the comb above that).

Chairs with plain turnings are not worth having at any price. A WINDSOR is merely a wooden chair, and unless it has some grace or merit it belongs in a modern kitchen. The cheaply, easily turned WINDSORS abound and often offend in rooms otherwise well furnished.

Windsor Chairs

THE twenty-three inserts in this little book are intended to make it more complete. The jacket is a writing arm chair in the Ives collection of Danbury. The two stools below on this page are in the same collection. The page of line engravings (88b) represents all the best standard styles of turnings, 107–110 being the Pennsylvania early type. Mr. J. H. Stiles of York, Pa., owns the chairs shown on page 88c, a remarkable eleven spindle comb, and on page 192, left, a very quaint and unusual chair. Page 88d at the top shows a three legged Windsor with T stretchers and an odd comb back with curved arm supports, both owned by J. Stodgell Stokes of Philadelphia. At the bottom of page 88d are chairs believed to be the property of Ex-Governor Sproul of Pennsylvania. They are unique and interesting. Page 192a shows part of a large number of Sheraton Windsors belonging to Mr. Mireau, Fountain Inn, Doylestown, Pa. Page 192b, right, shows a side chair with ears, in the Ives collection. Pages 192c and d are two fine chairs owned by Mr. Mireau, Doylestown, Pa. The carved arm chair (page 192 d) is a remarkably perfect specimen and the five spindle chair has a molded seat of very unusual character.

The chairs in this book from the Wallace Nutting collection have been dispersed.

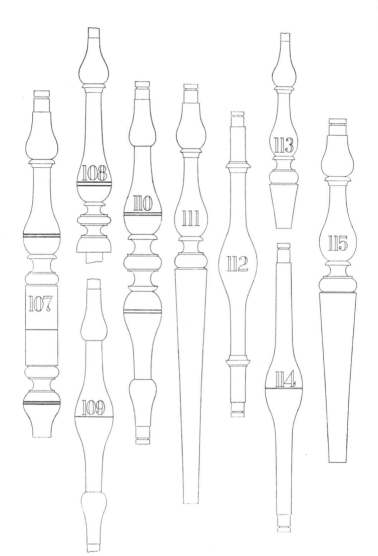

88b

88c

88d

One-piece Back and Arm Baby's High Chair

(ON TWO PREVIOUS PAGES)

Condition: Fine and practically original. One small, short spindle new.

Merit: The very highest. While we may question the structural wisdom of the one-piece back and bow, it is at least very graceful. We give two pictures of this beautiful chair that one may become intimately acquainted with its features, well worth study. The turned spindles of the arm, especially that on the right, is a very fine "fat" type. The seat is excellent, but the underbody is very worthy indeed. The beautiful turnings are the best type of the long, softly curving vase. The chair is twenty inches high to the seat, which we think is nearly an inch low for convenience, but probably something has been lost by wear.

It should be observed as a very important point that the turnings in the very best high chairs like this vary in no respect from the ordinary chairs, except in the lengthening of the plain, tapered lower end of the leg. In this chair and that which follows, the great bulb, the base of the vase and the top of the taper are fully two inches in diameter.

Date: Early.

Occurrence: Extremely rare.

Owned by WALLACE NUTTING, 32 Green Street, Newburyport, Mass.

The Quest and Value of WINDSORS

UNFORTUNATELY mere rarity gives a large market value to antique furniture. But the collector ought to discriminate and not be led astray by rarity, even by uniqueness, unless the piece in question has other obvious merits.

Historical chairs have very little additional value on that account. They appeal mostly to descendants of former owners.

Sets of WINDSORS, of good type, are so rare as to be desirable. Sets are very much sought for dining rooms in simple houses or summer houses. The late types are findable in sets but are not well worth owning. There was an infinite variety in the styles of turnings and in the sizes.

Cut-down chairs are not so desirable, their value being cut in half, at any rate if side chairs. As a slipper chair in a chamber an occasional sawed-off specimen may possibly be tolerated. The larger the chair the greater the value, if otherwise good. No refinished chair should be purchased at the price of an early original. The chances are a leg or two has been supplied or pieced, a top or spindles added, or the whole thing may be "synthetic," a hodge podge of several chairs. There is no objection to a new WINDSOR of good type, provided the purchaser knows what he buys and pays accordingly.

A shaky chair will require a considerable share of its value for repairs, and unless it is rare or fine it is worth very little.

Quaintness, a quality hardly definable, but felt only, and by the lover of it only, is a quality much to be desired.

Baby's Bow-back High Chair

Condition: Originally had a one-piece arm and bow, which failed at the sharp turn, and two arms have been substituted.

Merit: Very high, owing (1) to the nine-spindle back, (2) the well-shaped seat, but chiefly (3) to the remarkably heavy fine early turnings of the legs.

Date: Very early — before the Revolution.

Occurrence: Very rare.

Owned by WILLIAM F. HUBBARD, Hartford, Conn.

The Design of Little Chairs

Chairs for children or babes were often rather clumsy in appearance, for the reason that they were designed for rough uses. Many of them show wear from being dragged sidewise over the sanded floors. It is also impracticable to reduce all dimensions of the leg and back in proportion to the reduced seat, because the lines of the large chair itself were made as slight as strength permitted. It has been found in practice that the small turning at the neck of the vase cannot be reduced below a half inch without danger of breakage. It still remains for some designer to produce better effects in low chairs than have yet been seen. It requires greater care to make a small chair than a large one and the expense is greater. Hence only rarely do we find makers who dared to offer a chair for children which was at once delicate and elaborate. The author does n't remember to have seen such a chair with carved arms.

Baby's Bow-back High Chair

Condition: Fine. A minor split in cross stretcher. Otherwise original and very firm.

Merit: The highest. The turnings are rarely good, following perfectly, only in elongated form, the earliest and best vase type. The front arm spindles are also perfect.

The bow has an enlarged and neatly shaped footing or shoulder forming a kind of mortise and tenor, as it passes into the rail. This is sometimes seen in large chairs and is pleasing. The rare number of seven spindles (for a high chair) runs up to the bow, and they are carefully graduated in fan curves. There is a marked and pleasing flare to the entire back, in fine basket shape. The general effect of the chair with properly raked legs and full of graceful curves is very charming indeed. To save the owner from the last touch of vanity the seat, though neatly chamfered above and below, lacks the saddle effect.

Date: Very early.

Occurrence: Very rare indeed, possibly unique in the number of good details.

Owned by WALLACE NUTTING, Iron Works House, Saugus Center, Mass., a part of the "all WINDSOR," lean-to kitchen furniture.

Baby's Bow-back High Chair

Condition: Fine and original.

Merit: High. A somewhat lighter, smaller chair than the preceding, and therefore not admitting of turnings so deep. A good saddle seat; five gracefully fan-curved, long spindles, gracefully bulbous below.

Date: Early to middle period.

Occurrence: Rare.

Owned by ARTHUR LESLIE GREEN, Weaver House, Newport, R. I.

One wonders why high chairs are less carefully made now than formerly. Is it because we reverence children less? Or was the old chair well made because it was expected to serve for an even dozen children? At any rate, we cannot but be drawn to it.

Most baby chairs had a means of holding the occupant in. A wooden slotted bar was used, or a cord. Once placed, the youngster must abide the will of the higher power.

As that style of dressing children which imitated the garments of their elders was very charming, so low chairs made for children, in style like large chairs, are always attractive.

Some with only three spindles in the comb lack character. It is attention to the details in copying the large chairs, that gives the baby chairs their merit. None of these chairs originally had rockers.

The other low chairs shown on page 114 are later and less worthy.

The location of the foot rest varied considerably. The one here shown is very low and could have been serviceable only for a child of some size.

Baby's Bow-back High Chair

Condition: Good and apparently original, with the possible exception of a portion of the foot rest.

Merit: Very high owing (1) to the extreme rake and size of the legs, (2) to the method of the connection between arms and bow, (3) to the general quaint effect. The demerits are merely incident to the period, as these bamboo-turned legs are not so good as the earlier richer turnings.

Date: Late.

Occurrence: Very rare in so quaint proportions.

Owned by WALLACE NUTTING, Cutler-Bartlet House, Newburyport, Mass.

The Foot Rest on High Chairs

Many of the early high chairs had none. It was obviously the original intention to secure a child in the high chair, whereas the foot rest gave an opening by which an enterprising youngster could climb down. Further, there was more danger of oversetting the chair with the rest than without. Some chairs were made with adjustable foot rest to accommodate lengthening legs!

The clumsiness of the foot rests on chairs otherwise fine like that opposite leads to the suspicion that they were seldom original or if so that they did not stand the strain of time.

Bab'sy Comb-back High Chair

Condition: The two long side spindles had evidently been broken and badly mended by setting in new holes in the arm rail outside of the old holes. These are now restored to their original holes. The seat having split, two cleats were found as now, nailed under it. Otherwise original.

Merit: The nearly perfect type of its kind. The comb has the remarkable number of seven spindles, as in one other baby chair, a bow-back already illustrated. The author thinks the comb would have been finer for a deeper concave, to enable it to follow the back more closely as in the Stevens chair following. The turnings are the ball-foot type. The seat looked down upon is very fine, and the whole effect is charming.

Date: Early.

Occurrence: Very rare indeed, possibly unique in the sum of its good features.

Owned by WALLACE NUTTING, Iron Works House, Saugus Center, Mass.

List of Terms: *Underbody*

Below the seat is the underbody. The *turnings* are either Pennsylvanian with balls or with blunt arrow feet; New England, with vase and taper; bamboo, which is later; or a still later shapeless leg.

Stretchers or rungs: The horizontal pieces connecting the legs and one another.

Ball or bulb: The heaviest part of the vase or the bulbous center of the stretchers.

Rake, splay, slant: The slope of the legs.

Taper: That part of the leg extending below the vase.

Baby's Comb-back High Chair

Condition: Fine, apparently original.

Merit: Very high. The concave of the comb is deep, the spiral-carved ears and shape of the comb are very good. The legs are fair, but lose a grace they would have gained by tapering to a smaller end. The arm rail is a little heavy, but the seat is well shaped, and the general effect of the top is very good.

Comparing it with the previous chair, this comb is superior to that owing to its better curve, but this has six spindles to the other's seven. This chair is stockier.

Date: Early to middle period.

Occurrence: Very rare indeed.

Owned by SAMUEL STEVENS, North Andover (an heirloom).

High chairs suffered like their larger companions from being cut off at the bottom. A better reason existed in the high chair's case. As a child grew he needed less elevation to keep him in proper line with the table. So the poor chair suffered successive mutilations until, cut down to its bottom rung, it was finally discarded for the grown-up chair. Only occasionally the fine early symmetry and sentiment preserved it intact.

The height of the seat from the floor in babies' high chairs varies somewhat, but less than twenty-one inches is a pretty good indication that some sawing off has been done. The maker seems not to have dared to carry to the normal required length the rapidly spreading leg.

(a)　　　　　　　　　　　　　(b)

(a)
Baby's High Chair, Sheraton Scroll Back

Condition: Fine and original.

Merit: While the back rail seems suggested by the Sheraton chair back, and is graceful, it is sustained on flattened outside back spindles (Sheraton influence) which mark departure from exact WINDSOR style. The poorly—more properly thoughtlessly—shaped seat and the graceless sticks provided for legs mark degeneration.

Date: Very late.

Occurrence: Common.

Owned by WALLACE NUTTING, Cutler-Bartlet House, Newburyport, Mass.

(b)
Baby's High Chair

Condition: Original.

Merit: Slight. A poorer edition of the one following.

Date: Very late.

Occurrence: Very common.

Owned by WALLACE NUTTING, Cutler-Bartlet House, Newburyport, Mass.

Baby's High Chair

Condition: Fine and original.

Merit: The extraordinary rake of the legs makes it certain only a super baby could tip over in it. Yet the legs are not heavy, but have a humorous grace. This type in which the outside back spindles run above the rail indicate the beginning of the end of the Windsor style. Also the shape of seat. Good bamboo turnings, with the saddle.

Date: Very late.

Occurrence: The type is common, but not the fine underbody.

Owned by Arthur Leslie Green, Weaver House, Newport, R. I.

————

The Mystery of Style

There is nothing more puzzling in human nature than its lapses from the good to the bad in style as well as in morals. Place the good and bad style side by side and the bad will often be chosen, whereas another generation will strongly develop a taste for good form. The study of good forms, and comparisons to learn their merits are as necessary as any part of education. A sad reflection is that the good style is often more expensive than the bad, although the bad may cost more to manufacture.

One would suppose that the concentration of the manufacturers would tend to develop good taste because such concentration affords bases for comparison. But in practice the thing works out the other way. It is the lonely maker who shows genius. The more machinery the less thought in him who runs it.

Twin Babies' High Chair

Condition: Back legs restored.

Merit: As to style the chair has no merit. But it appeals
very strongly to sentiment and is a great oddity. Undoubtedly the proud father, presented with twins,
rushed away to create this piece as a great surprise to
the happy mother. No doubt it was successful as a
surprise, but scarcely in any other way, for the mother
would have said: "How cunning, but at table of course
we shall have to separate the twins as far as possible!"
Yet what a sight two tots would be in this double seat!

Date: Very late.

Occurrence: Unique so far as known to the author.

Owned by WALLACE NUTTING, Cutler-Bartlet House, Newburyport, Mass.

Construction of WINDSOR Chairs

The bow or round top was fastened to the seat by extending
away through it and being wedged. The central spindles, three or
four, were pinned to the bow, as also the bracing spindles, which
also were pinned to the tailpiece.

The two short spindles on each side did not as a rule run through
the bow.

The legs either pierced the seat and were wedged, or to gain
neatness did not quite penetrate and so their tops were concealed.

For the same reason the stretchers stopped short of piercing the
leg.

In some cases glue was used; in others dependence was placed on
wedges and tight joints alone.

Child's Comb-back

Condition: Fine and apparently original.

Merit: High. The height of the comb above the seat is nineteen inches. The chair is here shown large and there is no means of comparison on the page. But the seat is only ten inches high, proper for a child, not a babe.

Of course the turnings on a child's chair cannot be reduced in proportion to its size or it would soon be wrecked.

The carved ears, outsprung spindles, and the general features place the chair in a rank almost unique, for a child's chair.

Date: Early.

Occurrence: Extremely rare.

Owned by MRS. MORGAN G. BULKELEY, Hartford, Conn.

———

Child's Furniture

There is an age when children find themselves hampered by furniture too large or too small for them. As a rule furniture is made either for adults or babies with no step between. When therefore we do occasionally come upon a child's bed or chair or desk, it has all the greater charm, and the greater value from its rarity.

In the chair opposite we have an almost exact miniature reproduction of the large settee seat arm chair. Fear of weakness probably kept the maker from executing certain refinements which his taste suggested.

(**a**)
Double Bow-back

Condition: Apparently original.
Merit: Slight.
Date: Late.
Occurrence: Rare.
Owned by HERBERT B. NEWTON,
  Holyoke, Mass. *This applies
  to both chairs.*

(**b**)
Low Baby's Chair
Double Bow-back

Condition: Feet have been cut
  off.
Merit: Moderate, though the
  back is very well for the light
  type, and with its original
  height the legs would have
  been fair of the late bamboo
  type.
Date: Late.
Occurrence: Unusual.

Cradle with Bamboo Turning

Condition: Fine and original.

Peculiar in its suggestion of a *chaise longue*. As that is
a chair with seat drawn out, so this suggests a baby
chair drawn out.

Merit: High, owing to its grace and fine condition and the
good curves of head and foot and also of the side rails.

Date: Middle to late.

Occurrence: Very rare, possibly in these curves, unique.

Owned by ARTHUR LESLIE GREEN, Weaver House, Newport, R. I.

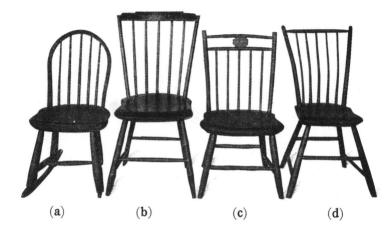

(a)   (b)   (c)   (d)

Low Child's Chairs

Condition: Good and original except (**a**) which has rockers added.

Merit: (**a**) is the best. (**b**) is of the "Sheraton" scroll back; (**c**) and (**d**) variations of the turned back rail.

Date: Late except (**a**).

Occurrence of (**a**) rare; others not unusual.

Owned by WALLACE NUTTING, Cutler-Bartlet House, Newburyport, Mass.

BEST EARLY SIDE CHAIR

BEST LARGE ARM CHAIR

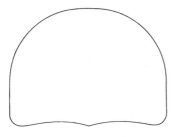

GOOD SETTEE SHAPE
PENNSYLVANIA ARM CHAIR

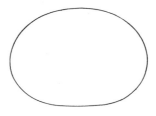

ELLIPTICAL SEAT
ARM CHAIR

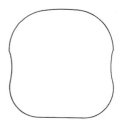

DEGRADED SIDE CHAIR

GOOD LATE SIDE CHAIR

Braced Bow-back WINDSOR

Condition: Original.

Merit: The highest, for its type. The turnings are very deeply cut, and the vase and ball strongly marked. The legs at their largest diameter are two inches, yet draw in suddenly and gracefully at the stem of the vase to seven-eighths of an inch. The stretchers are heavily bulbous, all alike. It is the perfect underbody of the earliest WINDSOR style.

The seat also, as in this type while having a strongly marked saddle, is chamfered away strongly at the sides (suggesting the use of these chairs for men who spread their knees well, and alas, probably tipped back).

Contrast this seat with the type which has two hollows for the legs.

The back is not quite so graceful as in later chairs, but the bow is still continuing in a curve as it enters the seat. This is characteristic of the earliest period. So is the shaved or whittled spindle with its slight bulb where it was held in the clamp or hand while being shaved or whittled from this point each way.

Date: Very early, 1725–1750.

Occurrence: Very rare with turnings as good. This is one of a set of six.

Owned by WALLACE NUTTING, Iron Works House, Saugus Center, Mass.

Braced Bow-back, Carved Bow

Condition: Fine and apparently original.

Merit: High. The blunt shape of the seat in front, without saddle or chamfer from below is a strange omission
in what is otherwise a good chair. The leaf pattern
repeated in carving on the face of the bow is a striking variation. The underbody is good.

Date: Early.

Occurrence: Extremely rare.

Owned by WALLACE NUTTING, 32 Green St., Newburyport, Mass. (The Cutler-Bartlet House).

Curiosities of Construction

One wonders why the upper bulb of the leg was so very high,
since grace suggests it should have been a trifle lower. The dissec-
tion of old chairs has shown that the hole for the leg was often
bored with a taper and the upper bulb was turned to a long, tapering neck and driven into the chair apparently as far as it would
go, thus forming a tighter joint.

The Rhode Island taper at the bottom of the leg arose out of the
deeply fixed notion that there is always beauty in curves. Good
taste approves a perfectly straight taper. The Rhode Island curve
begins somewhat above the line of the stretcher. In chairs made
from memory a very clumsy and sawed-off effect was produced by
making the leg largest at the stretcher line.

The ramp in the side of the seat probably arose from the desire
to lighten the chair wherever possible, which was also a primary
purpose of chamfering the edges on the under side.

Braced Bow-back WINDSOR

Condition: Good and original.

Merit: High. The stretchers are strongly bulbous but differ from the two preceding in shape. Seat not so good.

Date: Early, probably a little later than preceding.

Occurrence: Unusual.

Owned by WALLACE NUTTING, Webb-Washington House, Wethersfield, Conn.

Cushions

These may be made, as the housewife well understands, of various materials, but the most durable and substantial for a WINDSOR chair is leather. It should be cut to a good fit for the chair it is to serve. If leather is found expensive, its wearing qualities will show its economy in the long run.

Excellent cushions are also made from scraps of calico, gingham or chintz. The bottom of the cushion is usually made of bed ticking, and soft homemade cushions seldom have more than two pieces at the top and the bottom. The contents or filling of the cushion may be as various as that of beds. Our ancestors began with shredded cat-tails, with corn husks and with marsh hay. Later they used feathers and rarely hair.

A pair of tie strings should be attached at each rear corner to fasten around the outside spindles or bow. Comfort and beauty may thus be secured even with a seat of wood.

Braced Bow-back WINDSOR

Condition: Fine and original.

Merit: High.   Turnings fine.   Rings on cross stretcher.
Seat fine.

Date: Early, but slightly later than the heaviest type.

Occurrence: Unusual.

Owned by WALLACE NUTTING, 32 Green St., Newburyport, Mass.

———

The Original Cost of WINDSORS

One should not conclude that because WINDSORS have little or
no carving that they were therefore of little cost to produce. Good
turning is a slow process and accurate turning by hand almost impossible. As a test the writer watched a turner as he made a well-
shaped leg from a model. The wood, while maple, worked well,
but the time required was very long.

The wood of the bow must be nicely selected, without cross-grain,
or it will break, and sometimes this occurs in spite of all precautions.

It is a very nice matter also to secure a spindle of sufficient
strength and at the same time fine enough to enter the light bow
or comb. As a consequence factory-made WINDSORS always have
a coarse bow which compared with the old type is very woody.

The painting or natural finish of the chair is also an expensive
process. While a piano finish is not expected, soft surfaces are only
secured by rubbing. The nice surface of the old WINDSORS we
suspect was mostly secured through use, automatically so to speak.

Braced Bow-back WINDSOR

Condition: Fine and original.

Merit: High. This chair is the Rhode Island type of turning, the taper of the legs being hollowed. Also the ball above the taper is without a bead beneath it, as is usual. This turning, while fair, is not the finest. There are only seven spindles. Compare it with the chair following, which has nine. Seat fine.

Date: Nearing the middle period. Delicate chairs like this cannot be very early.

Occurrence: Unusual.

Owned by WALLACE NUTTING, Wentworth-Gardner House, Portsmouth, N. H.

———

The Bracing Spindles

The two bracing spindles in the chair opposite are correctly placed. No account was taken of these spindles in placing the regular spindles. That is, the holes for the bracing spindles were bored between the other spindles wherever space was afforded. In a few instances, where such chairs were made from memory, the maker erred in spreading his ordinary spindles or gathering them up to afford more room for the bracing spindles.

The effect is quite graceless and unnecessary. The tailpiece on the best designs tapers toward the chair and not away from it. That is, it is widest near its rear extremity. Its corners are either chamfered or rounded. The bracing spindles always penetrate the back completely and are always pinned or wedged to the back to secure rigidity. They should be of the same size and type as the other spindles.

Braced Bow-back WINDSOR

Condition: Fine and original.

Merit: With its nine spindles, fine rake of legs, delicate turnings, well-shaped seat, and light style, it is a very fine chair. Compare, however, the lower ball with the earliest heavy turnings, and it will be observed that a ring flush with the lower leg has been made a ball, larger than the lower leg.

Date: Middle period.

Occurrence: Unusual.

Owned by WALLACE NUTTING, Wentworth-Gardner House, Portsmouth, N. H.

An Exhibition of WINDSORS

The writer is glad to say that all interested in seeing the various types of WINDSORS may easily do so at the houses mentioned in the addresses below his name. Except in a very few instances the public will find examples of all the most meritorious forms, together with others somewhat inferior — above a hundred and fifty in all.

The oldest chairs appear in the lean-to kitchen at the Saugus Iron Works House. They are of the heavy type. The greatest number is to be found at Cutler-Bartlet House, 32 Green Street, Newburyport, where a little picture gallery is practically filled with them. But the other houses also have numerous fine examples. Students are at liberty to sketch in these houses to their heart's content, provided they do the owner the courtesy to procure his photographs rather than make their own. It is the intention not to forbid the diffusion of a proper familiarity with good lines but to encourage it.

Braced Bow-back WINDSOR

Condition: Fine and original.

Merit: Largely in the peculiarity of the saddle which in addition to the usual shaping at the top is also incised from below. The turnings are fair to good. The bow is a little heavy. Legs start too near the corner of seat. It has, however, nine spindles.

Date: Middle period.

Occurrence: Rare for saddle only.

Owned by WALLACE NUTTING, Cutler-Bartlet House, Newburyport, Mass.

A WINDSOR Revival

Of late there has been a diligent search for good WINDSOR furniture, especially in chair sets, settees, and comb-backs. So far as the writer knows there is not a set combining side chairs, arm chairs, settees, and stools. This is surprising in view of completeness that can be attained in richer styles of furniture.

It has become dangerous to the peace of mind of a country estate owner or that of a farmer's wife to leave a good WINDSOR on the porch facing a street. A fine limousine will stop for such bait, which is more deadly than the catchiest fly to a trout. In order to prevent as far as possible a revival of bad WINDSORS rather than good ones this little book has been written. Although the writer has studied the subject by fits and starts for years, he thinks the only proof of real knowledge of the lines of a good WINDSOR are to be found in reproducing it in a drawing from memory.

Braced Fan-back WINDSOR

Condition: Fine and original, except the huge bulb in the cross stretcher which does not fully agree with the rest of the chair.

Merit: Moderate. The turnings of the legs do not swell enough, showing decadence from the best type. The top-rail has not sufficient concavity.

Date: Middle period.

Occurrence: Braced fan-backs are unusual.

Owned by WALLACE NUTTING, Cutler-Bartlet House, Newburyport, Mass.

Owing to the favor in which fan-backs are held, together with the strength of the brace back, this style of chair is much sought for and is in every way very desirable.

The WINDSOR Settee

The scarcity of settees may easily be understood, as very large pieces of furniture are more difficult to preserve. Also the habit was common of placing WINDSORS in gardens, where neglect soon allowed them to fall in pieces. The best settee known was found in a hen coop. It will be impossible to discover one such old piece where a thousand are wanted. Nothing is rarer.

It is not usual to shape saddle seats in long settees, but a ten-legger will accommodate four persons provided the occupants are, as an Englishman said, "made according to act of Parliament." The usual lengths are forty-eight inches for two persons, sixty-six for three, and eighty-four for four.

Fan-back with " Horns "

Condition: Fine and original.

Merit: Moderate, but the chair is *Peculiar* in the small-ness of its seat, which is well shaped. One feels it may have been made for a half-grown child. Turnings ordinary.

Date: Middle period.

Occurrence: Unusual only so far as seat is concerned.

Owned by WALLACE NUTTING, Cutler-Bartlet House, Newburyport, Mass.

The Fan-back

Such a chair, to justify itself, should suggest its name. The spacing of the spindles must be very delicately done to secure grace. A sixteenth of an inch deviation from model is enough to spoil an otherwise beautiful back.

There is some confusion in the nomenclature of the fan-back. The practice in this book is to call a fan rising above an arm rail or bow a comb, and to use the term fan-back only in case of side chairs or of arm chairs which have no rail running around the back.

A matter of great importance in the fan-back is that the long outside spindle should be delicately turned. The vase shape is in this case necessarily greatly elongated and clumsiness is common. It will be observed that this turned spindle is a reproduction of the leg in miniature, except that it is a little longer. The turning at the large bulb and the base of the vase can hardly be more than an inch and three-eighths and at the stem it should never be more than five-eighths of an inch. Nine spindles beside the outside spindles are better than seven.

Fan-back WINDSOR

Condition: Good and original.

Merit: High. The ears are especially well done. The turnings are unusual and very good, but not quite the best.

Date: Middle period.

Occurrence: Unusual.

Owned by WALLACE NUTTING, Cutler-Bartlet House, 32 Green St., Newburyport, Mass.

———

Country-Made Chairs

Our fathers had the advantage of us in this, that the various sorts of native woods adapted to WINDSOR chair making were readily available to them. While oak can be made to do for the backs, hickory is superior for bows and spindles. It is getting more and more difficult to obtain. In fact, no native hickory is quoted in the eastern markets.

———

List of Terms: *The Back*

Spindles: The small, round pieces running from seat to top. Those below the arm at side are called short spindles. Chairs are called nine-, eight-, or seven-spindle backs.

Fan or *bowed* or *curved* or *spring spindles* refers to the spring outward, increasing each side of the center, of the spindles, in graceful chairs.

Sack Back: A name for double-bow backs.

Turned spindles: While all spindles are turned except in early chairs, the outside spindles of a fan-back, and the front spindles under the arm, are called specifically turned spindles.

High Fan-back WINDSOR

Condition: Good; original.

Merit: Unusual, owing to the fine height of the back. Turnings good   It is one of a pair.

Date: Early.

Occurrence: Rare, owing to height of back.

Owned by WALLACE NUTTING, Hospitality Hall, 89 Main St., Wethersfield, Conn.

Connecticut appears to be a good region in which to seek for unusually high-backed chairs. Perhaps the tradition that the inhabitants knew how to make things comfortable was well founded. At any rate, the higher the back the more comfortable the chair.

The effect of height is greatly enhanced by the nearly vertical back and the almost parallel spindles which should be very small and more numerous. The very high fan back seems usually to have blunt, uncarved ears or "horns," and in the instance before us they curve sharply. The seats of this sort of chairs look small, but are not. The effect of smallness and primness is produced by the height of the back.

These chairs are surprisingly light, and are striking in their effect in a set for a dining room where, more than elsewhere in a home, formality is pleasing.

What can one select to harmonize with such a dining set? The table that comes nearest to harmony is a light cabriole-legged Dutch foot table of maple, still easy to obtain at very moderate prices. Unfortunately such tables are usually rather small.

Round-seat Fan-back

Condition: Apparently original.

Merit: Hard to define, for one laughs rather than defines. Certainly the owner is to be congratulated on a very quaint possession.
The turnings often go with arm chairs, though the X-stretcher chair in the book has this sort of turning, and the writer owns a fine low-side chair with the same turning. The seat also is not uncommon with arm chairs. By omitting to chamfer the under edge of the seat, a clumsy effect is produced. The humor of the chair is largely in this omission.

Date: Early.

Occurrence: Very rare, possibly unique.

Owned by MRS. ANNIE B. HUNTER, Freehold, N. J.

Analogous Furniture

One who possesses a number of good WINDSORS meets the question of securing other furniture that will not clash with WINDSORS. Maple beds and tables, open dressers, and any eighteenth century turned furniture is suitable. Footstools of the WINDSOR style add much to the charm of a room and are always convenient for young or old members of the family. Braided or drawn-in rugs, pine pipe boxes, small wall cupboards and iron, rather than brass, fireplace furniture are complementary features.

Mahogany or the effort to imitate it in color is to be avoided with WINDSORS, for it spoils their simple, unpretentious charm. Further, no WINDSOR can be made strong in mahogany without using too much wood for good style. The consequence is that we see in shops mahogany WINDSORS clumsy and coarse as compared with the hickory and maple, the proper strong, simple woods.

Fan-back WINDSOR

Condition: Fine and apparently original.

Merit: Slight and neither in turnings nor seat, but

Peculiar in the almost half-circular concave of the comb.

Occurrence of comb rare; otherwise quite ordinary.

Date: Middle period.

Owned by WALLACE NUTTING, Cutler-Bartlet House, Newburyport, Mass.

Seat Shapes

On page 115 are shown a half dozen diagrams of WINDSOR seats. All of them are typical and not very rare. The seat of the chair on page 8 is far finer than the "best large arm chair." The tail-piece shown is usually narrower than this at the seat and widens as it grows. The settee-shaped seat is quite generally very large, really ample for a giant. It was the answer to a deep feeling on the part of a big man to sit at ease when his day's work was done. The seat called a "good late side chair" is the shape usually found in the bamboo type, a serious decline, but still good, and so far as the seat itself is concerned it is very good. The "degraded side chair" is the last and worst thing, such as was reached around 1830–1840, and still survives in modern chairs that are called WINDSOR.

Fan-back Windsor

Condition: Fine and original.

Merit: Slight. The spread of the back is wide, but the legs lack slant, being set too near the corners of the seat. Had they been placed correctly, and more boldly turned, the chair would be desirable. This chair is shown to indicate what to avoid and to point out what to seek.

Date: Middle period.

Occurrence: Not very unusual.

Owned by Wallace Nutting, Cutler-Bartlet House, 32 Green St., Newburyport, Mass.

Lost Examples

Several varieties of Windsors are either entirely lost or exist only as unique pieces.

Good "love seats" are extremely rare, and none that is of the best type is known to remain. The same may be said of six-legged settees. Only one or two perfectly shaped eight- and ten-leggers remain.

Absolutely satisfactory writing chairs there may be, but probably they are so only in the opinion of their owners. The perfect four-back chair has never been shown in museums. It may exist. When two hundred dollars was recently offered and declined for a very fine settee one may be sure such pieces stand practically alone.

Fine footstools and high stools are extremely rare. A set of six curved-stretcher side chairs is being held for three hundred dollars. Only individual side chairs of fine type are still to be had in numbers, with fairly common double-bow backs of the simple light type, and an occasional comb-back of good quality.

Braced Fan-back WINDSOR

Condition: Some of the set of six have had some back legs renewed and in one or two cases old legs are spliced.

Merit: High, considering the fine, early, fat turnings, combined with the brace back. The ears would be better if a little longer.

Date: Early.

Occurrence: Rare, as a set.

Owned by WALLACE NUTTING, Wentworth-Gardner House, Portsmouth, N. H.

The ear when not carved is sometimes called a horn; the term "horn-back chair" is sometimes heard in northern New England

---

Braced Fan-backs

This sort of chair is perhaps the most graceful among side chairs, and it is rare. For some reason the bow-back is more usual. In a small room the fan-back ears are apt to be in the way. The bow-back is no doubt the earlier style. The fan-back was the more easily constructed, and more durable. Even when the ear is not carved, it is, if small, attractive and very convenient as the temporary hook for a hat or garment.

Fan-back chairs as a remedy for colic may seem a startling suggestion. But the writer has more than once seen husky farmers double themselves like clothes on a line, over fan backs, while they rolled the sharp edges back and forth over the offending seat of colic. Their information is that the remedy is unfailing. It is here set forth as a suggestion, there being no extra charge for the prescription. One more reason to love the WINDSOR chair! We would point out that the scroll shape of the top-rail on the opposite page seems fitted to reach the seat of the difficulty. There can be no doubt that the experiment faithfully followed would cure the rugged, and WINDSOR chairs were not made for weaklings, anyway.

Braced Fan-back WINDSOR

Condition: Apparently original.

Merit: Moderate. But the piece is very interesting as an experiment. Its great oddity is the omission of heavy outside spindles. It is built up as if it were merely a comb! The bracing spindles would indeed save the back from weakness. Possibly the unusual and extremely wide tailpiece had something to do with that thought. The seat also is odd, suggesting the English, and without side ramp.

Date: Middle period.

Occurrence: Very rare.

Owned by J. B. KERFOOT, Freehold, N. J.

The Weak Point in WINDSORS

It is the back. This weakness is nicely overcome by the braced back, and in arm chairs the arms stiffen the back. The only way to secure strength in an unsupported back was by the use of elastic woods, otherwise a strain would mean a break somewhere. Well selected hickory or oak will bear a far greater strain than is ever likely to be put upon it, and what is better will spring to fit the strain. This is the peculiar merit of the American WINDSOR. If the chair falls over, its back will spring and not give way, and the lighter it is the less likely is it to meet disaster. This feature is unique in chair styles and can hardly be overemphasized. The idea of a springy grill is really of double purpose — to add to comfort and to resist abuse.

A VARIANT OF CHAIR ON PAGE 134

Pennsylvania Fan-back

Condition: Fine, but legs are cut down.
Merit: Moderate. Spindles too coarse. Comb fine.
Date: Early to middle period.
Occurrence: Unusual.
Owned by WALLACE NUTTING, 32 Green Street, Newbury-
port, Mass.

Fan-back WINDSOR

Condition: Rail mended, but all original and strong.

Merit: High. Seat good; turnings good, with hollowed taper near the bottom of legs. Nine spindles and a high back, but plain ears.

Date: Early.

Occurrence: Unusual.

Owned by WALLACE NUTTING, Wentworth-Gardner House, Portsmouth, N. H.

Spacing of Spindles

The chair opposite is a good example of the added attractiveness of numerous spindles, as well as added comfort. It is obvious that the more spindles the greater is the comfort, only it must also be borne in mind that as spindles increase in number they should decrease in size, otherwise the back will be too stiff, and so counteract the very effect sought.

The space of two inches is all that should ever be allowed between centers of spindles at the seat, and an inch and three quarters is the least space allowable. This slight difference varies the effect greatly. The close spacing allows a fan spread higher up without separating the spindles there so that each appears lonely.

The size of the hole in the seat should never exceed seven sixteenths of an inch and never be less than three eighths of an inch.

Fan-back WINDSOR

Condition: Fine and original.

Merit: Very high indeed. An almost perfect specimen of light side chair. The turnings are especially fine. Notice the true vase shapes and the deep cuts, which give emphasis to the bulbs. The only thing we could ask which we have not in this chair, is carved ears. The seat is perfect, and the concavity of the fan top, or rail, sufficient to give comfort and grace. The chair is airily light.

Peculiar in the very fine point to which the feet run down.

Date: Best middle period.

Owned by MRS. M. E. WELLES, Wethersfield, Conn.

Fine Points of Style

In the chair opposite the seat shows the middle period by being left somewhat high at the sides in front and hollowed under the sitter's legs. This is a handsome effect — more so than the earlier type. If, however, the hollowing of the seat is strongly done, and the legs are placed well in from the sides they must pierce the seat, as they will occur in its thin portion. This chair is somewhat of a compromise.

The bottoms of the legs in any good WINDSOR side chair extend well beyond the seat, vertically considered. Hence the WINDSOR, in .ddition to being the lightest chair, is also the most stable on its base.

There is a wonderful likeness in the chair opposite between the turnings of the legs and the side spindles. It is this thoughtful matching of styles which gives a chair great charm.

Fan-back with Comb

Condition: Fine and apparently original.

Merit: High, as the little comb is not only a convenient head rest, but adds much to the grace and quaintness of the chair. Indeed, one at first wonders why more chairs were not made this way, till one sees readily that the same thoughtfulness that suggested this chair would carry one on to add also the arm in which form we usually find it.

Occurrence: Very rare.

Date: Early.

Owned by E. R. LEMON, Wayside Inn, So. Sudbury, Mass.

A Comparison

Had the next previous chair had nine light spindles and a secondary comb, lower than the chair opposite, the result would have been very beautiful — a perfect expression of the best WINDSOR features in their daintiest form. Probably no such exquisite specimen exists.

A question about carving arises both in this chair and in the arm chair with double or tandem combs. In the only specimen the writer has seen of carving on both sets of ears it seems rather overdone. It would seem to be in more subdued taste to carve only one set of ears, which set seems immaterial.

The height of the secondary comb should be sufficient to form a head rest. Anything higher would seem grotesque and top heavy. In this instance a somewhat higher lower comb and consequent shortening of the secondary comb would have added grace.

Bow-back, Seven-spindle WINDSOR

Condition: Fine and original.

Merit: Moderate. Comparing it with other chairs, one sees that it falls behind the best bamboo in character, in the number of the spindles and the lack of the bulb on them; also in the slightly inferior legs.

Date: Late period.

Occurrence: Common.

Owned by WALLACE NUTTING, Framingham Center, Mass.

The horseshoe back is graceful in the drawn-in sides, before the bow enters the seat. Also the seat is well formed.

————

Good Late Chairs

This sort of chair, and that immediately following, have the best general contour of the late WINDSORS. To be consistent, however, and in better style, the spindles should be turned in bamboo fashion, as in the chair on page 66. Thus the legs, stretchers and backs would agree.

The bamboo turning of the underbody is undoubtedly a very great declension from the beauty of the vase style of turning. In part good makers made up for the falling away from grace by carrying the bamboo effect into the upper body. Thus the pure bamboo chair is harmonious throughout, whereas the vase turning of the finer type has no repeated element in the upper body to correlate all the parts of the chair.

The stretcher on the chair before us looks precisely like a piece of bamboo, but unhappily the legs are less perfect and the top forgets the idea altogether.

Nine-spindle, Bow-back WINDSOR

Condition: Fine. A set of six, one of which has had a bow mended.

Merit: High for the period, owing to the perfection of the back, and the good seat, and the good taste of the bamboo of the underbody. The back is a fine example of fan spacing, and the bow has an attractive in-sweep at the sides characteristic of the middle period. The spindles appear to have been hand-shaped. If we are to have the bamboo turning of legs, this is a good example.

Date: Late.

Occurrence: Not very unusual for single specimens; rare for a set of six.

Owned by WALLACE NUTTING, Webb-Washington House, Wethersfield, Conn.

Constructional Terms

Dowel. The rounding of the end of a piece of wood as of the end of the bow so rounded to enter a bored hole in the seat is sometimes called a dowel. Broken or shortened legs are repaired or extended by running a true dowel into the two portions to be joined.

Pin. The name of the little hardwood pieces which pass through the bow and the top of a spindle and secure the top, reinforcing or dispensing with glue.

Stretcher mark. A fine turned line on the leg to mark the spot where the stretcher is to enter. This is incised on the lathe to secure uniformity and save subsequent measurement.

Glue groove. The groove turned near the ends of stretchers and tops of legs to hold the glue as they are driven home.

Curved Stretcher Bow-back

Condition: Fine.

Merit: High. It consists largely in the construction of the underbody, with a curved stretcher in front and spoke-like stretchers meeting it from the rear. The shape was probably called out by the curved bows of the upper part of the chair giving the suggestion of the curved stretcher. Like many inventions it may have come by accident. The bow and the seat are graceful, and the chair is large.

Date: Late period.

Occurrence: Very rare.

Owned by H. HILLIARD SMITH, Hartford, Conn.

The chair is large enough for an arm chair. A feature of great rarity is the carving on the bow in the form of an interrupted flute. Chairs with the curved stretcher are the greatest rarity and are much sought for.

The Lore of the WINDSOR

The lure is a larger subject than the lore. The writer has sought to gather in this handbook all that is known of the WINDSOR, but it is astonishing how little that all is. If the reader will, however, observe the suggestions made, he will be saved from being an easy mark for the faker. At present many new to collecting are buying with avidity chairs made for and only worthy of the kitchen and placing them in positions of honor. They are also buying new chairs for WINDSORS which are not so. Under the stimulus of fashion they forget that a new-fashioned shape cannot give satisfaction, because our fathers tried every conceivable variety of turned stick-leg furniture. No graceful line has been added. We would beseech buyers to take care lest the result of zeal without taste should be ridiculous.

Nine-spindle, X-Stretcher WINDSOR

Condition: Fine and apparently original, barring slightly shortened legs.

Merit: The back is good, the seat well ramped but lacking saddle; turnings poor; but an interesting peculiarity is an X stretcher of great oddity and really amusing in its originality. One of the stretchers was made large enough to allow the other to pass through it.

Date: Late.

Occurrence: Very rare; possibly this very form of stretcher is unique.

Owned by ARTHUR LESLIE GREEN, Weaver House, Newport, R. I.

The X Stretcher

The question whether the X stretcher is desirable bears looking into. It cannot have balance, as appears in this chair, where one stretcher is different from the other. Most readers will agree that the bulbous stretchers arranged as usual in the form of an H are a feature of no little attraction. Probably also the ordinary stretcher is somewhat stronger, as it enables the leg to resist side strain.

There is an X-stretcher WINDSOR in possession of Trinity College, Hartford; but such chairs seem not to have won popularity. A symmetry now lacking in the X stretcher is said to have been attained by running four stretchers into a small hub, neatly turned, but the writer has not seen such a chair.

Braced Circular-back, Arm WINDSOR

Condition: The feet below the turnings have been spliced; and the left arm is not original.

Merit: As a WINDSOR, depends on the definition. If a chair can be a WINDSOR without a spindle back, except for the bracing spindles, then this chair is of high merit, for it is very attractive. The turnings are fine. There can be no doubt regarding the originality of the back as there are no holes in seat or bow where spindles have been. The chair is thoughtfully made and is no mere freak. Apparently the maker derived his suggestion from a mahogany chair, perhaps a Heppelwhite. The flattened spindle or splat was decorated.

Date: Early middle period.

Occurrence: Perhaps unique. Certainly the writer never saw its like.

Owned by WILLIAM F. HUBBARD, Hartford, Conn.

A branded name is sometimes found on the under side of a WINDSOR seat, but usually on late chairs. Advertisements of WINDSORS showing rather crude cuts are found in newspapers during the latter half of the eighteenth century, mostly about the time of the Revolution. They show good vase turnings. These notices are in sufficient numbers to prove the widespread use of the style. Many thousands of WINDSORS have been consumed as firewood, along with more pretentious furniture.

"Sheraton" Back, Double-rail Windsor

Condition: Fine and apparently original.

Merit: The turnings of the underbody are good for the bamboo type, but were not carried out in the back. An added feature is a bulb to receive the lower member of the double rail, and a top-rail which is sustained by overlapping the outside spindles. The middle stretcher is too small for the side stretchers. The chair has some attractiveness.

Date: Late.

Occurrence: Very rare.

Owned by E. R. Lemon, Wayside Inn, South Sudbury, Mass.

———

Furniture Labels

This chair, bearing a label on the under side of the seat, affords an opportunity to study dates. The labels on furniture are rare, but when found are important and highly interesting. This label is from an engraved plate of good size, though a part of the paper has rubbed through, but there remains to serve as a frame for the text a handsome and elaborate high post bed, with fine draped canopy, of the Chippendale period. At each side are chairs, apparently upholstered Chippendales. The reading matter is between the posts to this effect:

"Richard .... Jr., Upholsterer Makes Couches .... easy chairs, French chairs, Bedsteads, chusin [sic] seat chairs, puts up .... trimming, silk, tapestry, paper Hangings .... New York 1771

Orders (?) from Country and beyond the sea carefully executed."

Before the "New York" was a name probably of the engraver and this line apparently applies to the date when the label was made, rather than when the chair was made. We see, therefore, that these fine, almost ideal turnings were made at least about as late as the Revolution. Reasoning forward in time and comparing other chairs of approximately known date, it is highly probable the label was used in this case in the decade in which it was made.

Cut-arm, Bow-back Windsor

Condition: Fine, original except possible slight shortening.

Merit: Chiefly in its peculiarity of the cut arm. The object was undoubtedly to secure a light, strong construction with an arm but (a) without carrying a rail around the back and (b) without a weak attachment of arm to a spindle in the usual way. The result was a chair, simple, easy to make, light and strong.

Date: Middle period.

Occurrence: Very rare.

Owned by Arthur Leslie Green, Weaver House, Newport, R. I.

Size of Windsor Seats

Very early side chairs had a width of seat of sixteen and a half to seventeen inches, at the widest point, while the piece was ordinarily made of a two-inch plank, and was left fully or nearly that at the thickest parts when finished, to give the necessary strength. The depth (front to back) varied greatly, but less than fifteen inches is too shallow and more than twenty-one inches too deep for comfort or style.

The width of arm chairs may run to twenty-five inches or any comfortable proportion.

The great variety in size of seats even for grown persons indicates that chairs were often made to order and possibly even to measure! In some neighborhoods a side chair with a small seat is called a "lady chair."

Heavy, Low-backed WINDSOR

Condition: Good.

Merit: Chiefly in that it is

Peculiar in the arms and legs. It also carries a stretcher behind. The turnings and curved-arm supports are in English style.

Date: Difficult to fix. We feel that the setting of the legs so near the corners points at least to an English model.

Occurrence: Very rare.

Owned by ARTHUR LESLIE GREEN, Weaver House, Newport, R. I.

Factory WINDSORS

The writer recently visited a large modern WINDSOR factory, filled with many thousands of chairs. The backs were about as good as could well be produced at the selling price, which did not admit of refinement. But a great improvement of the underbody was easily possible without increasing the cost. The exhibit was a proof that the public is not discriminating; that few seek after beauty of line.

In fact in the faculty room of a great American University the chairs — and there are many — are reproductions of the poorer English type, and quite discreditable to the management. Yet this university has many professors teaching arts, crafts, design, architecture, etc. One of our greatest public libraries is also furnished by a notable firm of architects with chairs of mongrel pattern and bad construction, weak where they should be strong, and extremely clumsy and heavy in the arms.

Double Turned-Rail Comb-back

Condition: Legs cut down and rockers added.

Merit: This bamboo-turned chair lacks much grace in the underbody like those of its period. There is an odd comb, with sprung spindles.

Date: Very late.

Occurrence: Of comb rare, otherwise common.

Owned by RHODE ISLAND SCHOOL OF DESIGN, Providence, R. I.

————

Where WINDSORS Were Made

It is not known how the American WINDSOR was developed, but it originated in Philadelphia. It is rare in the South and, if found, is an obvious importation from the North. The term "Southern" applied to WINDSOR, therefore, means, or should mean, a Pennsylvanian or New Jersey origin. The straight taper below the turning on the leg is a New England feature, except in Rhode Island, where the taper is concaved.

The writer has found very few WINDSORS south of the Potomac, and those few could often be traced to northern origin. English WINDSORS, except of recent importation, are rare in America, for the reason that as a rule only fine furniture was imported, the simpler sorts being made here.

Jersey WINDSORS followed generally the Philadelphia types, with minor local peculiarities.

Bow-back WINDSOR

Merit: This piece is included as an oddity and a suggestion which shows that the builders of WINDSORS ex-
perimented long to find a graceful effect. For instance,
had this chair had from one to three more spindles and
a consequent widening of the back we should have the
type settled upon by the usual maker.

The *stool* or cricket calls our attention to the fact
that most stools are WINDSORS. In this case the idea
is well carried out with the side and middle stretchers.

Date: Late.

Owned by ARTHUR LESLIE GREEN, Weaver House, Newport, R. I.

The Bead on WINDSOR Bows

It usually consists of two fine grooves cut on the front face of
the bow, one near each edge. In rare instances the entire space is
covered by a single wide flute or concave. In poor modern reproductions where the bow is too heavy this flute has been overworked
and enlarged until it bears no semblance to the proper style.

The back of the bow is usually rounded to give lightness. Occasionally we find a bow of a perfectly round section, especially as
the second bow on light arm chairs, but the style is not so good.

Breaks in the bow at the point of spindle borings are common.
They could only be avoided by careful selection of straight-grained
wood, and more careful bending.

The bow passed entirely through the boring in the seat and was
secured by wedging. The spindles seldom passed entirely through
the seat. To find them passing through is to excite the suspicion
of a new back.

Flat-spindled or "Sheraton" WINDSOR	One-piece Bow-and-arm Comb-back
Condition: Somewhat poor.	*Condition:* Cut off for rockers.
Merit: Ordinary. Has the side back spindles extended beyond the others.	*Merit:* The top is graceful. The underbody the ordinary late bamboo turning, with no character.
Date: Very late.	*Date:* Late.
Occurrence: Common.	*Occurrence:* Common.
Owned by WALLACE NUTTING, 32 Green St., Newburyport, Mass.	*Owned by* WALLACE NUTTING, Newburyport, Mass.

Ten-legged, Triple-bow-back Settee

Condition: Fine and practically original.

Merit: The highest. The turnings of the legs are perfect for the medium weight. The ramp and scroll of the arms are very handsome. It will be noticed that the middle bow has nine spindles and the side bows seven each, and that these are all arranged with a fan spread.

Date: Early.

Occurrence: Extremely rare.

Owned by VICTOR A. SYKES, Hartford, Conn.

Dream Settees

The above piece was taken to the last world's fair and is the best the writer has seen. Yet there are what he must call dream settees. For instance, there is said to be one with the back bows extending to the seat. And the informant had seen it. Another had seen a braced-back settee! These are things to unearth for a future edition. Meantime the present piece and the one following are interesting enough to cause danger of infringing the tenth commandment. And they are handsome enough to cause the inquiry, why don't we find "love seats" of this type? How utterly charming they would be!

Three-bow-back, Eight-legged Settee

Condition: In this plate recent diagonal braces have been worked off. As may be seen three rear legs are substitutes.

Merit: The highest, owing to the general design, the closely set spindles, the high bows, and the excellent arms.

Peculiar in the great width of the seat, a full two feet, just a third of the length. Compare this with the previous plate, showing ten legs in which it appears that for symmetry an eight legger must as in this case have all its legs rake.

Date: Early.

Occurrence: Very rare indeed.

Owned by the MISSES MABEL and ELEANOR JOHNSON of Hartford, Conn.

The bows of the back are halved into each other where they cross, and the center bow is higher than the side bows. Also the spindles under each bow are made in reference to it, spreading in delicate curves, thus giving a "three-chair back" as real as in a Chippendale settee.

178

Scroll-back, Ten-legged Settee

Condition: Fine, one slight mend at connection of an arm with end spindle.

Merit: Very high. The back is well done. The center spindle, matching those at the ends, gives pleasing distinction. The style of the arms, however, shows a latish date, and a decadence from the style which has a sidewise scroll and a turned spindle at the front, corresponding with that at the back. The legs, while well turned for bamboo, especially the stretchers, do not win upon us like the earlier turnings.

Date: Late.

Occurrence: Rare. This piece passed out of the hands of the writer, to his great present regret, before he began to collect or value WINDSORS.

Ownership not known.

There has been a recent strong revival of the WINDSOR settee. Its appropriateness on our long modern porches has made itself observed. The length of its back allows some play of taste. Thus we have in the settees the two types, bow and fan, which we found in the chairs.

Ten-legged, Heavy Low-backed Settee

Condition: Fine, original.

Merit: Moderate. It is pleasing, but simple and without distinction.

Date: Late.

Occurrence: Fairly common.

Owned by WALLACE NUTTING, Cutler-Bartlet House, Newburyport, Mass.

———

The WINDSOR Settee

This naturally developed from the chair, just as other styles of settees were derived from corresponding styles of chairs.

One form has a heavy back continuous with the arms, which in the better styles are scrolled and wrought into knuckle ends. The same remarks made regarding style in the turning of the chair apply to the settee. The attraction of the settee rests largely upon its presence with a set of chairs. The mind is thus led along to feel the effort at harmonious style through the different articles of furniture.

Six-legged Settee

Condition: Good and original except for cleat under one end, and possible shortening of legs.

Merit: A graceful piece. Legs of ordinary merit, stretchers unusually good.

Peculiar in the attachment of the arms. The bow of the back runs down into the seat and the arms are attached by a long splice to the bow. Arms are very neatly carved.

Date: Late, as shown by bamboo of front arm spindles, and the legs.

Occurrence: Very rare.

Owned by THOMAS B. CLARK, New York City, N. Y.

————

The Short Settee

This style has won strongly on the imagination of lovers of WINDSORS. It would be too much to peer into the mind of the original maker, but doubtless he "had his reasons." These courting chairs are much sought for, not only owing to the name but because they are not too long to serve with chairs to form sets. The longer settees are better adapted to the hall or a porch.

Comb-back "Love Seat"

Condition: Fine and apparently original, except long
  stretchers which do not match the end stretchers.
Merit: High. The piece has a style all its own. The seat
  is finely shaped as a double saddle. The turnings of
  the legs are odd but end with the blunt arrow. The
  turnings of the spindles are also elaborate. These spindles
  match the large arm spindle except for size. The arms
  sweep well out, but are not carved. Pennsylvanian.
Peculiar especially in its comb back, extremely rare, lacking ears, however.
Date: Probably early period.
Occurrence: Very rare, possibly unique.
Owned by Mrs. Wm. Raedake, Providence, R. I.

Low-back Love Seat

Condition: The curious legs are hard to understand, as they differ so entirely from the front arm spindle.

Merit: The piece has a heavy arm, without carving, but the seat is cut with a double saddle. The legs are slightly fluted on the taper. They are unsatisfactory.

Date: Middle period, probably.

Occurrence: Rare.

Owned by ARTHUR LESLIE GREEN, Weaver House, Newport, R. I.

"Sheraton" Back Late WINDSOR Settee
(ONE OF A PAIR)

Condition: Fine and original.

Merit: Slight, but nevertheless the piece is interesting. Obviously it was made by one who had seen a Sheraton chair back. The arrangement of the legs is also interesting, being merely two chair bases set at the ends. The turning is bamboo throughout; the seat is ramped at the end; but the piece is odd in having no arms.

Date: Late.

Occurrence: Rare, possibly unique.

Ownership: Photograph supplied by C. R. MORSON, Brooklyn, N. Y.

Bow-back "Love Seat"

Also called John and Priscilla chair, courting chair, short settee, double-seated WINDSOR, and in Connecticut sometimes even wagon chair — but wholly without warrant.

Condition: Fine and apparently original, except some slight reduction of the feet, and a caveat as to the long stretcher.

Merit: High. Though the seat is plain and the leg turnings not the deepest, the back shape is good, and the piece very worthy.

Date: Middle period.

Occurrence: Very rare.

Owned by ARTHUR LESLIE GREEN, Weaver House, Newport, R. I.

"Sheraton" Square-back "Love Seat"

Condition: Fine and apparently original.

Merit: Moderate but good of its type. The style of the back, the plainness of the spindles and legs, the arms, precursors of the "Boston rocker" all indicate a

Date: Very late.

Occurrence: Rare as are all "love seats."

Owned by RHODE ISLAND SCHOOL OF DESIGN, Providence, R. I.

Compare this piece with the chair on page 76.

HIGH DESK CHAIR. NO MERIT

High Desk, Turned-rail WINDSOR

Condition: Good. The front rung appears as if renewed.

Merit: Not classifiable. Bamboo turnings, plain seat (as often in late types) but

Peculiar and really humorous in its grand-pa-long-legs effect.

Date: Late.

Occurrence: Very rare.

Owned by ARTHUR LESLIE GREEN, Weaver House, Newport, R. I.

The Child's High Chair

The quaintness and merit of a WINDSOR high chair is largely in the wide splay of the legs. There was no danger of such a chair tipping over, however obstreperous its occupant might be! Compare their style and dignity with the latest, lightest type on page 104. In this latter the poor fan top was the easiest way out as a substitute for the fine bow or ear.

High Stools

Such stools are very common in shops, before or behind counters, and are WINDSORS, though of a much-debased type. If there ever was a graceful example the writer has never seen it.

Maud Muller's milking stool was a true WINDSOR, and its handle was an extension of the seat like the tailpiece of an extension-back WINDSOR!

WINDSOR Three-legged Table

Condition: Apparently original.

Merit: High. The stretchers are good but the legs are not heavily turned. The merit of this sort of table seems to have been overlooked or the early makers would have left us more examples. The light weight and the grace of the piece, made in harmony with chairs in the same room, are features worth gaining. It was natural to insert the stretchers at different heights, in a three-cornered piece, to avoid weakening the legs. But that was frankly done in the very early three-cornered chairs and stools.

It is of course necessary to form the top of a thick piece of pine to gain a solid hold for the legs, otherwise battens would be necessary and they would contravene the theory of a WINDSOR piece which is a "stick leg." The top would properly consist of one piece of pine which would limit one to a small table, unless one were fortunate enough to find some of the old thirty-inch pine. The edge of the top could be chamfered underneath, gaining the effect of lightness as in chairs.

Date: Early to middle period.

Occurrence: Unique so far as the writer's knowledge is concerned.

Owned by L. G. MYERS, New York City, N. Y.

Windsor Table

Condition: Good and original.

Merit: Moderate. This is a true WINDSOR table, if stick legs, turned, with splay and stretchers can make one. The turning, it is true, especially of the stretchers, is heavy and graceless, and properly there should be no cleats.

Date: Early, perhaps very early.

Occurrence: Very rare.

Owned by WALLACE NUTTING, Iron Works House, Saugus Center, Mass.

These tables suggest the question, because of their obvious advantages, why they do not oftener occur. Other styles of chairs have their corresponding tables, etc. Why not the WINDSOR chair? There seems no answer. A very attractive table could obviously be made in the style with handsome legs and cross stretcher to connect with end stretchers.

In the turnings the first makers of WINDSORS had the gate-leg table as their nearest and best model, and comparison with such a table shows many a similarity of line in the leg.

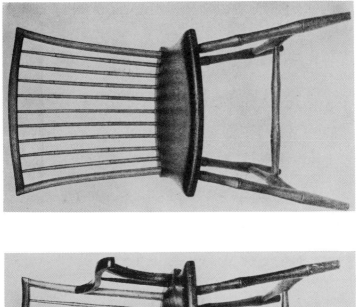

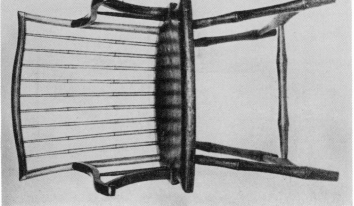

192a

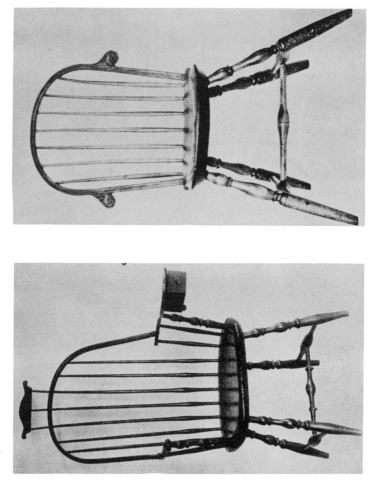

192b

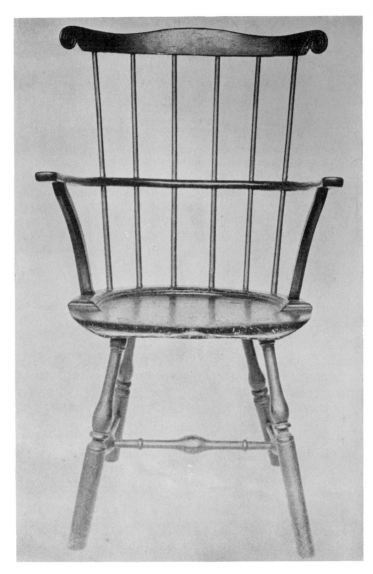

192d